"*The Box of Life* is a powerful tool for anyone seeking to live a purposeful and meaningful life. With thought-provoking questions and practical advice, Orit Ramler helps readers connect with their true selves, uncover what is most important to them, and leave a lasting legacy. If you're looking for a way to lead an authentic life with a profound impact, this book is a must-read."

Dr. Marshall Goldsmith, *Thinkers50* #1 executive coach and
New York Times bestselling author of *The Earned Life,*
Triggers, and *What Got You Here Won't Get You There*

"Orit Ramler is a gem! This world-class executive and leadership coach has applied her insight, experience, and skills to the personal domain of how we live our lives and capture our essence. This practical book offers an approach that can be truly transformational. We often do not realize what we have or what we have done until we take the time to collect what matters to us and what we have experienced—both positive and negative—by reflecting on our own experiences and our ability to positively affect others. Filled with examples, compassion, and humanity, *The Box of Life* guides us to think more deeply about our life. But rather than waiting until the end of life to reflect on and appreciate what is important, this book helps us to start now and be more intentional about what we do and what we leave as our legacy. This is a book everyone should read and take to heart."

Sim B. Sitkin, the Michael W. Krzyzewski University distinguished
professor in Leadership at Duke University, copresident of the Behavioral
Science and Policy Association, president of Delta Leadership, editor of *The
Routledge Companion to Trust,* and coeditor of *Organizational Control* and
The Six Domains of Leadership

"Replete with heartwarming stories, inspirational ideas, and practical advice, this book will invite you to reflect on—and preserve—what matters most in your life."

Dr. Tal Ben-Shahar, founder of the Happiness Studies Academy and *New York Times* bestselling author of *Happier*

"This book is filled with inspiration, depth, and magic, and reminds each of us that we are filled with inspiration, depth, and magic, too. If you're looking for a fun and fascinating way to make sure you capture what your life is all about, then *The Box of Life: A Guide to Living with Purpose and Preserving What Matters Most* is for you!"

Deborah Grayson Riegel, author of *Go to Help: 31 Strategies to Offer, Ask for, and Accept Help* and columnist at *Harvard Business Review*

"What's more enticing, more captivating than a box of treasures? Perhaps one that captures your life, your memories, your stories, your questions. Orit Ramler's vibrant entrepreneurial spirit and compassionate coaching skills shine throughout this jewel of a book, as she shares stories, raises questions, and helps us consider what matters to each of us as we create, layer by layer, our own deeply meaningful boxes of life."

Betsy Polk Joseph, coauthor of *Power through Partnership: How Women Lead Better Together*

"Using the lens of a single man and his efforts at the end of his life to preserve his legacy, *The Box of Life* offers the reader an emotional 'permission slip' to delve into their own memories and curate those life moments to outlast their physical lives. Consider this as a workbook. Orit's executive coaching skills shine through in the structure of the chapters, helping the reader to take small, reflective steps along their path to capture their personal legacy. Be sure to 'reflect and take actions.'"

Ellen Goodwin, cofounder and CSO of Artifacts

"A careful review of the book reveals a stunning observation—life must be lived in a manner that savors who we are, where we come from, and recognition of what really matters in our personal life journeys. Orit Ramler provides sorely needed wisdom and focused reflection to all of us in need of greater clarity and purpose as we examine the meaning of how best to live and experience our lives."

Vincent Guilamo-Ramos, PhD, dean and distinguished professor,
Duke University School of Nursing,
and vice chancellor, Nursing Affairs, Duke University

"*The Box of Life* doesn't just remind us how precious our memories are, it shows each of us how we can transform the smallest things into our greatest gifts: stories. Jewish tradition constantly urges us to remember, and this book gives us practical advice to help our loved ones carry us forward."

Rabbi Daniel Greyber, author of
Faith Unravels: A Rabbi's Struggle with Grief and God

www.mascotbooks.com

The Box of Life: A Guide to Living with Purpose and Preserving What Matters Most

The author has tried to recreate events, locales, and conversations from their memories of them. In order to maintain their anonymity in some instances, the author has changed the names of individuals and places, and may have changed some identifying characteristics and details such as physical properties, occupations, and places of residence.

Although the author and publisher have made every effort to ensure that the information in this book was correct at press time, the author and publisher do not assume and hereby disclaim any liability to any party for any loss, damage, or disruption caused by errors or omissions, whether such errors or omissions result from negligence, accident, or any other cause.

Cover Photo Credits:
pics five
Bruce Amos
dp Photography
Marina Shvedak_nice foto
Treenoot

For more information, please contact:
Mascot Books, an imprint of Amplify Publishing Group
620 Herndon Parkway, Suite 220
Herndon, VA 20170
info@mascotbooks.com

Library of Congress Control Number: 2024900965
CPSIA Code: PRV0224A
ISBN-13: 978-1-63755-840-9

Printed in the United States

This book is inspired by and dedicated
to my eternal friend, Charles Stern Z''L.
May his memory be a blessing.

"I never kept a diary, but I was loath to destroy the paper trail of my life. The drawers of my desk and the file cabinets were stuffed to capacity with the pieces of my life. At ninety years of age, it was time to clean the house. I stuffed a small box, then bigger ones, and finally placed my squirreled-away life in a box that had once held ten reams of paper. I came to the realization that there, in that box, was the story of a wonderful life."

Charles Stern to Orit Ramler

THE
Box
OF
Life

Orit Ramler

A Guide to Living with Purpose
and Preserving What Matters Most

MASCOT
BOOKS
an imprint of Amplify Publishing Group

Scones (A pa recipe)

... Salt
... Card ? Soda
... Tartar

...olden Syrup
... sour milk (if fresh milk used
Tartar ro 1 teaspoon to milk + Syrup
...yers, beat ... roll aside ½ hr at least.
... stand aside of cut. Drop
... milk card of cut.
...espoons cook both sides,
...bbles appear.

Contents

Foreword

The world was at a standstill, and so was I. Recently retired and rendered housebound by the pandemic, I decided it was time to reckon with things I had to put on the back burner while working, traveling, and taking care of all those *other* things that required an immediate response. So, in June of 2020 I undertook the cumbersome chore I'd avoided for eight years.

Fifteen file boxes filled with documents, articles, lectures, reports, cards, letters, taxes, medical records—removed from my late parents' desks and file cabinets—were still sitting in storage, taking up precious space. Being an only child, I already had the letters meant for me and the keepsakes, the art, dishes, photos, furniture, and the important legal documents and records. But what would I do with the ephemera of my parents' lives? What would I do with my own?

Although they had pared down their belongings as they grew older, I do believe my folks kept every paper that touched their hands, particularly my mom. Dad was adept at filing, and his files were voluminous. Mom's had labels only she understood and were overstuffed with whatever she wanted to put away at that moment in time. (This was a mutual source of irritation, as they occasionally worked on projects together.) So, my home became the repository for my parents' archives, and I became the reluctant archivist and shredder. The path down this paper trail was overwhelming, both emotionally and physically. What if I missed something important? Something sentimental? Something valuable, even? I had endured the grieving process long ago, but what if it started all over again?

My relationship with my parents was a powerful one: often challenging, always loving. For the last ten years of their lives, we lived in the same town again, and they died just four months apart after a marriage spanning almost sixty-five years. I knew there was a lot of life in those boxes, and I spent a long time going through them. But I didn't cry until I was nearing the end of the task and received an unexpected email. It was from a close friend of my dad who said, "I finally completed the project I promised your dad before he left us."

I had forgotten that he had given his friend a box too. It was quite different from the ones I inherited. It was curated. Her box contained *only* items he mindfully and tenderly placed there to tell the story of Charles M. Stern. All my sorting, shredding, and recycling was a duty discharged, and, by the end, I saved the equivalent of one box of papers. Orit's work was truly a labor of love and perseverance, and, ultimately, she had written a book that fulfilled more than a promise. I received the completed manuscript the next day, and I wept with happiness.

The Box of Life Project was inspired by my dad, but it is much more than the story of a life. It's about the families, friendships, and communities that shape us. It offers a practical, original way to collect what you wish to pass down to your own loved ones and a means of parting with those things you can (and probably should!) discard along the way.

I am thrilled to see his wisdom and humor reflected in these pages. And

I am so grateful to Orit for the friendship they shared and for the sisterhood she and I now share. And Charles, I'm certain, is delighted that his spirit lives on.

—Ina Stern,
daughter of Charles Stern

Orit and Ina

Introduction

"If there ever comes a day when we can't be together,
keep me in your heart. I'll stay there forever."
—A.A. Milne

My phone rang. A voice on the line said, "Please come see me. I would like to say goodbye. My time is running out." It was my friend Charles, uttering the words you never want to hear from a loved one.

Later that day, I knocked on his door, and for the first time in the twelve years I'd known him, he didn't open it for me. Instead, a caregiver ushered me in. Charles was sunk comfortably into his couch, still looking polished and handsome as always. I kneeled next to him as he grabbed my hand and held onto it.

In an effort to minimize the reality of why I was visiting, I asked him his favorite question: "So, what's your next project?"

Charles was a creative entrepreneur who was always working on something, perpetually on the quest for his next idea. Gently, he replied, "I don't have any, because a project that can't be finished is not a project. You must always finish what you start."

As the meaning of his words sank in, we sat in silence. I knew at that moment that my friend's physical presence was coming to an end. Charles without a project was like an oak without sunlight.

After a few minutes of ice-cold silence, he turned his head to me and tightened his grip on my hand in a loving, trusting way. "But you have one big project that I gave you, and I know you will complete the task."

I nodded, reassuring him that he did still have a project, through me, to which he smiled, once again squeezing my hand. "I will be watching over you."

A while later I said my goodbyes, and although deep inside I knew it was the end, I left believing it was *his* goodbye, not mine, because I was sure I'd see him again in a few days. We often choose to believe things in order to keep moving forward.

Two days later, on September 17, 2012, while I was on my way to Washington, DC, for a meeting, Charles's daughter, Ina, called to let me know that he had passed. I had to stop on the side of the road as tears blurred my eyes. Charles left earth peacefully at his home after living a full ninety-two years of life. The day he left was Rosh Hashanah (the Jewish New Year), a day in which we celebrate new beginnings. And although his death represented an ending, for me it was also the start of something: the project he left for me.

It was important for Charles that his journey wouldn't end the day he physically departed earth. He believed that leaving a legacy of our life's stories is something we owe to those who were here before us, and to those who will follow. But most importantly, we owe it to ourselves.

It was also important for him to live his life with purpose and meaning. He expected everyone to live that way. Whenever I found myself overwhelmed and navigating life on autopilot, he would look me straight in the eye and say, "Orit, focus on living." *Focus on living* was one of his favorite sayings. Charles aimed to never "waste" a day in his life. His motto—*the secret to longevity is to be creative and always have a project*—served him well.

Charles had a plan for everything to make sure it would meet his high standards of a purposeful life; he even planned his goodbye. He also planned a way to ensure that he would not only be remembered, but people would actually learn even more about him once he was gone. Here I am fulfilling that plan.

Charles was a doer; *execution* was an important word for him. Like Charles, I am usually a "do it now" kind of person. My urgency to do things right away can drive my thoughtful husband insane. But I'm an Israeli; I was born in a tiny country struggling for survival. After a few years in Israel, I spent my childhood moving from country to country—six different countries before the age of thirteen. At a very young age, I learned that *tomorrow* is sometimes too late. But in the case of Charles's project, I kept delaying. I'd tell myself, "As soon as I finish X, Y, and Z I'll get to it," or "This is not the right time." Almost a decade has gone by since the day I assured Charles that his project would be fulfilled—ten years too long to fulfill my promise.

Perhaps it is true that, as Ecclesiastes puts it, "For everything there is a season and a time to every purpose under the heavens." I've reached a season in which I've developed a peace of mind that can only be obtained at a certain stage in life. My kids are finally independent young adults. My executive coaching career is strong. Most importantly, I've reached a season in which Charles's project has suddenly become more relevant and urgent. My own vulnerability has become obvious to me. I've had two upper-cervical fusion surgeries. I need glasses if I want to read anything. I can't sleep twelve hours (or even eight) like I used too. Osteopenia is knocking on my door. And the list goes on and on.

I've grieved the painful loss of my beloved dad, my mother-in-law, and friends who left us too soon. My mother and my friends' parents are like candles, melting in front of me, slowly but inevitably shrinking away. In this season, if I don't want more family legacies to be forgotten, as so many have, it's time to write this book. I'm in the season where finding meaning and purpose—which, as Charles said, we should be in constant search of—has become a mandate, not an option.

On top of everything, months of isolation due to COVID-19 granted me extra time to think and reflect and presented me with existential questions that usually hide behind the hustle and bustle of daily life. The pandemic confronted me with the reality that we are mortal and things can end rather abruptly. It is up to us to preserve our own history, to share what we have learned, and to protect the future of our families and humanity as a whole. It is also up to us to live every day being the best version of ourselves.

In my late fifties, I have come to understand that life doesn't wait for us to be present or ready—it goes by fast, we are all vulnerable with no exceptions, and purpose is what matters.

I write this book with the hope that it helps others the same way it helped me. I emerged more committed to living with purpose and meaning while building a tangible legacy worth remembering for generations to come.

Charles, by sharing your story with me and inspiring me to write *The Box of Life*, I was made more aware of my own story. And by writing this book, I'm making others eternal too. Our lives are now intertwined for eternity, my dear friend.

Chapter 1

A Friendship That Led to an Idea

"The unexamined life is not worth living."

—Socrates

I first met Charles in 2002, when he visited the offices of the Durham-Chapel Hill Jewish Federation in North Carolina. I was the director of what was then called the Jewish Community Center Without Walls. Charles was approximately five feet tall with a stocky build, snow-white hair, hazel eyes, and a gentle, low-baritone voice. He looked to be in his eighties. I was in my midthirties.

He and his wife, Mildred, had just relocated from San Antonio, Texas, to be closer to their only child, Ina. As a newcomer to the area, he had reached out to us with hopes of meeting people in the community and finding volunteering opportunities. I had just moved to the area from Argentina four years prior with my husband and two kids.

From the day we met, despite our almost fifty year age difference, we clicked. We felt a deep connection that led to a lasting bond. We had many things in common, from our aligned values, interests, and creativity, to our stubbornness and the passion with which we lived life. We both always spoke our minds, believing that honesty is the healthiest way to go. We also shared our high standards and expectations for ourselves and others. I admired his life philosophy, attitude, principles, and the fact that he always seemed at the helm of his life and circumstances.

A few months after I met Charles, my good friend Bryna nominated me to become the executive director of the Durham-Chapel Hill Jewish Federation, and Charles was fully supportive of that. People often see qualities in us that we don't see ourselves, and when they push us out of our comfort zone, they are giving us a gift. Although our friendship was young, Charles passionately wanted me to get the job. He believed in me! He made the point to come see me almost every day to give me tips during my preparation for the interview process.

While I was getting ready to make my presentation as one of two final candidates for the position, Charles gave me a paper clip to carry in my pocket because he knew I was a nervous public speaker—especially in my second language. He confessed that although he loved being the center of attention, he himself always carried one.

"Every time you get nervous, gently pinch yourself with the paper clip, and you will be distracted from your anxiety and pulled into the present," he said.

I got the job as Charles hoped I would. Years later, I found myself giving a paper clip to my son when he ran for treasurer at his high school. He won his election.

A few years into my position as executive director, Charles joined the Federation's board. He was passionate, stubborn, and always eager to take us to the highest standards of excellence. Working with him was not easy. He would start every sentence by saying, "As we did in San Antonio, we . . ." and someone would always reply by saying, "We are not in San Antonio." Charles had a knack for finding flaws in everything, but most importantly, he would always come up with a solution. He would speak his mind but with respect. For me, it was a treat to have someone who would always remind us that in the good old days, they used to do things this way or that way. The past is a good teacher, for there is always something that can be learned from it. Charles called it like he saw it. One thing led to another, and my friendship with Charles became bigger and richer.

When I stepped down from the Federation in 2009 to start my own coaching and consulting business, Charles was disappointed, as he had appreciated my work and enjoyed visiting me there, but he understood that it was time for me to move on. He was proud of my accomplishments and excited about my new projects. His encouragement and approval were very important to me.

Once I left the Federation, my friendship with Charles evolved into frequent phone calls, in-person visits, and attending the plays he produced. We would discuss life and its meaning, current events, and share the million creative ideas that each one of us had on any given day for making the world a better place.

Charles's Wish

On a rainy morning in 2011, Charles told me, as he did at least every other week, that he had an idea for a new project. Only this time, I was part of his project. He asked me to come see him at his and Mildred's new apartment in Chapel Hill.

"There's a terrace filled with artificial flowers to help people find the place. It makes it look cozy while avoiding the need to water real plants," he explained as he gave me directions. He added, "That's part of accepting that I'm aging and can't do everything I did before, but I can still enjoy the beauty of what makes me happy." I had never liked artificial flowers, as I grew up with fresh-cut flowers that my parents loved and had grown with care in their garden, but I came to appreciate them after hearing Charles's reasoning. Now I have artificial flowers on my desk as a reminder that as I get older, I too can find ways to enjoy what life offers me today.

As soon as I walked into the two-bedroom apartment, I savored the essence of books, music, and art. The home felt familiar. Perhaps it was the natural warmth, or Mildred's little purse draped with a handkerchief that immediately reminded me of my grandmother. Charles led me from the living room into his grand office. It was filled with books, new and old, and a large, old-fashioned desk. He looked as if he were the king of the world, an image accentuated by the big, beautiful rings on his wrinkled yet firm hands.

After offering me a hot cup of tea and freshly baked cookies, Charles made his project request. "I want you to convey to the world who Charles M. Stern is."

What? He wanted me to write his memoir? Charles explained that at his age, ninety, it was hard for him to type. He had a program that would transcribe spoken words, but it was not very accurate. He was busy working on many projects—reassuring me that "having a project or two is the secret to longevity."

But me? I explained to him that I was honored that he had thought of me, but that I was not the person to write anybody's memoir. To start with, English was my second language. Although an accent doesn't come through in writing, incorrect grammar and limited vocabulary do. Additionally, I had no prior experience with writing memoirs, and I was busy launching my business as a personal and professional development coach. And further, I was in a tireless battle with immigration law in order to bring my parents into this country. Plus, I had two teenagers at home, two dogs, and a husband who was often traveling for work.

After listening to me plead my case, Charles casually laughed softly, as if I had said nothing of importance. "Never be embarrassed of yourself. I want you to write the way you talk, because that's the only way you will sound like yourself. That's your voice and I want your voice telling my story. The way you speak is part of your charm. It is representative of your authentic way of being," he said. "And I don't want someone who has written a memoir before. I prefer someone who knows me, who gets me. It would be easier for my daughter, who is a professional publisher, to say good things about me.

I'm her dad. But I want another perspective, so people know who I really am." He didn't even bother to challenge my other excuses about being busy. Charles knew that when we find meaning in a project, we make time for it, and he believed I would.

I compromised and told him we would start meeting and see where this would take us. I didn't promise anything concrete because I didn't want to disappoint him, but I said we'd give it a try. I knew that if anything, I was doing a *mitzvah* (a Hebrew word that roughly translates to "commandment" and is interpreted as "a good deed") by visiting and listening to his stories. Furthermore, I also knew I would be learning something new every time we met.

It ended up being much more than that.

In our first couple of meetings, Charles brought his childhood back to life. I was beginning to appreciate the power of personal stories and how they can teach us so much about a person and ourselves. Then, in about our third meeting, Charles gave me a large, heavy cardboard box. The box was worn, and I could tell that it had been with him for quite some time. Handing it to me, he said, "Orit, you now have my life in your hands." The box suddenly felt even heavier. "Go home, open it, and tell me what you think." It was pouring outside and as I lugged it into my car, I protected that box with my whole being.

Once home, I turned on some classical music and sat by a window, letting the calming sound of the rain soothe me. I was shaky and anxious. The words "You have my life in your hands . . ." echoed through my head and still do to this day.

As I opened the box and started digging, I felt like an archaeologist, though instead of excavating land, I was excavating a man's life. Like an archaeologist, I reached into the box not knowing what I would find, and then I had to put the pieces back together to tell a larger story. I was trying to complete a complex puzzle without having a final picture as a reference. My father was an archaeology buff. When I was a child, he took me to many famous sites in Israel and throughout Latin America. At the time, I didn't enjoy my father dragging me to those places, but as an adult, digging through that box and piecing everything together, I felt a wave of appreciation.

So what did I find in Charles's box? In short, I found a life story. I found a clear view of Charles's soul and essence. There were hundreds of papers: love poems, birthday greetings, newspaper clips, photographs, recipes, pink slips, congratulation notes, thank-you notes, quotes, speeches, a family tree, charity pamphlets, and medical records. These papers together illuminated Charles's values, beliefs, dreams, hopes, and ideals. The box spoke of his intense love for his wife, his devotion to his daughter, and the many hats he wore. It was a testimony that writing and the visual and performing arts were his passions. He was without doubt a voracious reader, thriving on discussion and debate. I saw how he went from success to failure and from failure to success. As he explained to me later, the box to him was "just" a collection of "important materials" from his life. To me, it was much more than that. I had only met Charles for the first time when he was in his early eighties, but his box gave me a window into decades before that. Inside the box was a whole life.

I felt overwhelmed. I looked at and spent time with every item, connecting the dots and learning more about how Charles became the person he was. After many hours, days, and even weeks putting the pieces of the puzzle together, I started to see the picture emerge. This box did not only give me a factual view of the events of Charles's life; more importantly, it showed *how* he lived his life.

I remember calling Charles and telling him, "That's our book!" I explained to him that his box conveyed who he was more than any other thing we could envision. His box was his memoir.

"Archaeology holds all the keys to understanding who we are and where we come from."
—Sarah Helen Parcak

Just a glimpse into Charles's box and life

A New Project Emerges

That powerful moment when I dug into Charles's box shook me. As I started the process of writing this book and honoring my promise to Charles by letting the world know who he was, one thing became clear to me: we all need a box, or more specifically, a *box of life*. That's when the Box of Life Project was born.

I immediately started thinking, "I want to pass my life stories to others as well. I don't want to just leave some financial assets and real estate after my death." I also started asking myself, "Would I have so many unanswered questions about my ancestors if I had their boxes? What am I putting in my own box?"

Since then, I've created my box and started coaching others in putting their boxes together. There is value for every person in creating a box—a curated series of remembrances that encompasses the richness of our lives. A box that contains choice items that reveal a life story—the highs, the lows, the pivotal moments, the essential relationships, and more. As a result, the Box of Life Project is an expansion of Charles's box—it includes what I learned from reviewing his box, from making my own, and helping many others create theirs.

This book is an invitation to create your own box—to sift through memories and mementos, seeking what's truly important to you and tells your story. Imagine one day, one hundred years from now, someone opens your box. What will they learn? What will they find about how you lived your life?

My Box of Life

What I've Learned

While writing *The Box of Life*, I've coached those wanting to build their boxes, read a multitude of books and articles on the subject of memories and preservation, and spoken to entrepreneurs and experts specializing in both the preservation of life stories and the pursuit of living meaningful lives. Thanks to my friend Charles's life story and legacy, and by working on the Box of Life Project, I came to the conclusions below, all of which I hope to address with this project:

- For so many families, stories and legacies are being lost forever.
- Many artifacts, mementos, and heirlooms (photographs, videos, art, jewelry, etc.) are kept and preserved. However, the stories attached to them are almost always lost. When passed from one generation to another, without the accompanying story that gives them meaning, these priceless items are demoted to "stuff," "clutter," or "junk." Eventually, they end up in a thrift or antique store, if not the garbage.
- The items that are kept are not usually organized; they are all over the place and many times no one knows where they are. Boxes, drawers, attics, basements, and even digital solutions like the cloud quickly become overwhelming from the number of items stored in them whose meaning is not explained.
- Social media offers the opportunity to share ourselves, but many people present only one dimension of their lives.
- Human beings are social creatures—we have a need to build communities and to feel a sense of belonging. This only became more apparent during the recent global pandemic that isolated all of us from one another. We want to feel connected and part of something greater than ourselves.
- Elderly people desperately need a vehicle to reduce isolation and loneliness. Reviewing their own life stories can be a therapeutic activity and a source of hope and comfort.

- Younger generations are searching for purpose, looking into their souls, and increasingly taking interest in their roots and family stories as a compass to guide their lives.
- Our elderly are dying, or their memories are starting to fade. Along with them, our history is being buried.
- It is time to take action!

What's in This Book for You?

As you journey through the pages of this book, you will find the following:

The science behind the Box of Life Project. I share my research findings that explain why box building can be such a meaningful and impactful pursuit. I talk about how our memory works, the role that stories and nostalgia play in our lives, and more. My intention is to provide a strong foundation to understand the benefits of creating a Box of Life.

Extracts of what I found in Charles's box. You will learn about a wise, creative, and resourceful man who lived a very full life. When opening Charles's box, it was like opening a treasure chest filled with valuable lessons we can all learn from.

Reflections on my findings. From each item I uncovered in Charles's box, insights on how we live our lives emerged. I share these along with anecdotes, philosophies, and lessons from my personal life, along with a glimpse into my own box.

Insights from others. While writing this book and coaching others on building their boxes, I engaged in fascinating conversations with people I knew and with strangers who are no longer strangers. By learning what they wanted to put in their boxes, I came to understand them through a new, deeper lens.

An invitation to reflect and a guide to start creating your own Box of Life. As you navigate this book, I invite you to pause and reflect on your true essence and life story. Have a place to take notes, record your thoughts via audio or video, and answer the questions you will find throughout the book. As the philosopher Edmund Burke stated, "To read without reflecting is like eating without digesting." You will also find guidance and suggestions that will help you create your own Box of Life.

The Box of Life Is for All Ages

Charles's box emerged toward the end of his life, and it's natural to think of a box as a legacy. But creating a Box of Life is a valuable activity throughout life.

If you are in your twenties or thirties, beginning to put together your Box of Life will encourage you to reflect on your purpose and how you are investing your time. The box will reconnect you with your roots while helping you to think about what you want your life story to ultimately be.

If you are in your forties, fifties, or sixties, you likely have many memories and artifacts spread all over the place. Creating your Box of Life will encourage you to consolidate them and reflect on your journey. It's an opportunity to take stock of your life and determine what's *missing* from your collection. Perhaps there are areas of your life that need refocusing, or dreams that have not yet been pursued. You can begin to shape your years ahead and legacy in a more focused direction.

If you are in your seventies or beyond, this is an invitation to start collecting all those scattered memories. If you find anything is missing, now is the time to add it and do those things that matter the most on your bucket list. This is a chance to reconnect with memories that are important but have faded over time. It is time to tell the story of your life.

If you have an aging family member, sit with them and build their box with them. You'll find it rewarding not only for them, but for you too.

If you lost a loved one, this is a chance to collect their belongings and ensure their story lives on forever.

If you have kids, start their Box of Life so nothing in their story gets lost. When they are old enough, they can take over the project.

It is not pleasant to think about our own mortality. Traditionally, at the end of our lives, we all have just one box: a coffin or an urn. However, building a Box of Life ensures we will have two boxes. And while our remains are preserved in the first box, in the second box—the Box of Life—our soul's essence is preserved. It is a box that serves us personally and will inspire, teach, guide, amuse, and tell stories that transcend time. It is a box that invites soul searching and promotes soul sharing.

When I told my friend Daniela about this book, she said, "Every man is a common man until someone writes about them." Most books about people focus on celebrities or public figures with exceptional accomplishments. This book is about what was revealed to me by the box of a common man. It showed me what's important in life, both during the journey and after—what we leave behind. Once you look into someone's Box of Life and see the richness of their story, you realize the word "common" does not apply to anyone.

Daniela also reminded me that we die twice. The first time is when we take our last breath, and the second time is when we are forgotten. With this story, Charles and all who build their Box of Life will never die a second time.

"Preserve your memories, keep them well,
what you forget you can never retell."
—Louisa May Alcott

Chapter 2

Creating Your Box of Life

"The longer you can look back, the further you can look forward."
—**Winston Churchill**

The rainy day that Charles told me I had his life in my hands, my own life deepened. The more I dug into Charles's box, the more I wanted to reconnect with my roots and the most essential parts of my life. It inspired me to rescue family stories that otherwise might be buried, so they could be passed forward from generation to generation. More importantly, it inspired me to help others go through the same process. The impact of doing such a thing enriched my life beyond anything I ever imagined. I often wonder if Charles was intentional about the priceless gift he left for me, and if he knew what kind of impact it would have on me. Asking someone to write a book about you may be viewed as a selfish request; perhaps it was actually selfless.

As soon as I shared the idea for the Box of Life, I started receiving unexpected emails, texts, and calls from people telling me they had started "boxing." I must admit, I was amused by the use of the term and happy to bring a new meaning to a verb that I previously associated with a painful sport, dog breed, or men's underwear brand. Now people were using the term in a whole new context. A young man named John wrote, "Hey, Orit, I just boxed an epic date with my girlfriend." Katherine, who is in her forties, eagerly told me, "I'm boxing this book that I'm reading which is changing my life." "Can you help me think of a gift for my granddaughter that will be worth boxing?" asked Martha, who's in her seventies. And "happy boxing" was even the closing to a few of the emails. I realized in these moments that the "Boxing Movement" had been born.

Getting Ready to Box

I hope that you will feel inspired by Charles and other "boxers" to start creating your box—or at least understand the merit behind the exercise. I come back to Charles's full life and other heartening life stories in the chapters that follow, but in case you decide to start boxing as you read, let me help you get started.

Each of our boxes should answer five fundamental questions:

1. Who am I?
2. How am I living my life?
3. What's most important to me?
4. How do I want to be remembered?
5. What do I want to pass on to generations to come?

These are big questions! For most of us, they are not something we can answer off the cuff. Doing so involves a journey of awareness and discovery. Your recommended packing list includes

- a mind open to working with whatever this evolving journey may reveal to you;
- the willingness to take a trip that links your past, present, and future;
- the courage to accept that you're human and not creating the box of a superhero.

You also need a few physical items—particularly a place to record your thoughts as they emerge. This could be a notebook, smartphone, or computer. You may also want a physical box or container and folders that you can label.

There Are Many Ways to Box

The goal of creating a Box of Life is to dust off treasured mementos and memories, collect them in a meaningful and tangible way, and use them to tell a life story. It doesn't have to be yours. In addition to boxing for yourself, you can

- box for your parents or older friends and relatives,
- box for your kids,
- create a box for a lost loved one,
- help someone put their box together,
- make a box as a gift for a special occasion.

No Excuses Accepted

While most people I've encountered are enthusiastic about boxing from the get-go, others have had some hesitations. I compiled all the issues I've heard from people who were initially hesitant about boxing and what we learned together. If you're telling yourself that boxing may not be for you, the following might address some of your concerns:

"I don't have any interesting stories in my life to box."

Wrong. We all have a unique story, and each one of our stories is interesting in its own way. You might think your story is just "one more story," but no two people have the same life experiences. Have you met any human being whose life is not interesting? Can you honestly say that there is nothing to learn from your life?

"I can't remember the past in detail." Don't stress about getting every little fact straight. No one is expected to remember their past perfectly—we are not wired that way. Try to reconstruct your memories as accurately as you can; that is good enough. What you remember is your truth, and that's the story that you box. Physical items may instinctually spark meaning, even if the specific details around the memories are blurry, so these can still be worth boxing.

"I don't have family." We all do, even if they are not blood relatives. Humans are our descendants on a large scale. Anne Frank didn't have direct descendants, yet the diary she kept has enlightened millions around the world.

"I don't have information or anyone to ask about my past." No problem. Use the internet to do some research and build on the little information you have. Plus, you can focus on what has meaning to you now. Again, no need to aim for perfection. Something is always better than nothing.

"I'm not sentimental." You don't need to be a sentimental person—or a hoarder, for that matter—to box. Boxing is also about letting go (covered further in chapter 15). To box, you need to care about living with purpose and sharing whatever means the most to you.

"I'm lazy." I promise you that you will be energized by the journey, and the sooner you start, the easier it will be. In this book you will find tips that will help you create a habit of boxing. You will start breaking it down into smaller chunks and boxing as you go. You can also find a boxing cheat sheet on page 275.

"I don't want to revisit my past." Always remember that our past has helped shape our present, and *present* is a synonym for *gift*. If there are memories you want to avoid, remind yourself that these are just shadows of whatever you have experienced in the past. Boxing can be healing. And if you're very firm on not looking into the past, that is okay too. You can start boxing from today onward, as it is never too late for a fresh start.

There's no question that building your Box of Life can be an intense experience. For me, going through my past and curating what is important to my story was a roller coaster of emotions. At times I felt sad or wistful, at others joyful about rediscovering happy memories. Overall I felt a sense of satisfaction as I reflected on my life. And starting my kids' boxes was an intense yet comforting experience. It was intense because I was trying to determine what to put in their boxes while wondering whether what was important for me was also important for them. It was comforting because it was like watching a movie playing from the day they were born through all sorts of milestones. I encountered so many things that we forget add meaning to the present day, such as the many drawings of dogs that my daughter collected since preschool (she is now a dog lover and has earned both a master's in anthrozoology and a certificate in Animal Assisted Therapy) and a picture of my two-year-old son with his first plastic golf set (he is now a scratch golfer). In the end, putting a Box of Life together is a journey that invites us to look back at our lives and regain purpose in looking forward.

The Bird, the White Canvas, and the Puzzle

Charles, a writer and artist himself, reminded me a few times that "the most difficult things for writers and artists are starting and ending their piece." The same applies to our life story.

It can be a daunting task to reflect on our life story and sift through the many boxes we likely keep with old photos, papers, and mementos. They are probably scattered everywhere, including the darkest corners of our attics and basements and in the many applications and files we keep on our devices. So how to begin?

Charles began his box with information about his parents. I started mine further back, with my grandparents. Unfortunately, most of the valuable information about their lives left with them. How far back can you go?

Over twelve years ago, when I was pivoting into coaching, I hired my own coach to help me get started. She noticed I was stuck, paralyzed by the many goals and ideas I had, even before the starting line. She recommended I read Anne Lamott's book *Bird by Bird: Some Instructions on Writing and Life*. The title refers to Lamott's father's philosophy. As a child, Anne's brother was overwhelmed by a huge school project on birds. Their father's advice was, "Bird by bird, buddy. Just take it bird by bird." One step at a time. *Bird by bird* became one of my mantras.

Charles also noticed my tendency to become overwhelmed by my passions and projects. He read me a quote from Vincent van Gogh that I later found in his box. The quote is from Letter #464 to Theo in 1884, and it reads: "You don't know how paralyzing that is, that stare of a blank canvas is, which says to the painter, 'You can't do a thing.' The canvas has an idiotic stare and mesmerizes some painters so much that they turn into idiots themselves. Many painters are afraid in front of the blank canvas, but the blank canvas is afraid of the real, passionate painter who dares and who has broken the spell of 'you can't' once and for all."[1] Charles loved the idea of a white canvas; he saw potential in everything and would never shy away from an invitation to be creative. He believed that once you start, you flow. To him, flowing was the main goal when engaging in any activity. But for me the blank canvas was overwhelming.

---

[1] Cited as appeared in Charles's box and can be found at the Van Gogh Museum, www.vangoghmuseum.nl/en/highlights/letters/464.

If, like me, you enjoy putting together jigsaw puzzles, you might know that there are several tricks that can help the process go faster and with less frustration. The principles behind those tricks worked for me when I was exploring Charles's box and building mine. After I open a puzzle box, I do my best to sort the pieces into groups while turning them over. For example, if I'm putting together a puzzle that depicts the ocean with a boat and seagulls flying around, I create a pile of pieces for each object in the picture. First, I might make a pile of ocean pieces, and if the ocean has different shades of blue, I create sub-piles within that ocean pile. Then I create piles for the boat, the seagulls, and the sky. As I'm doing so, I also create a pile of all the edge pieces. Once I'm done sorting, I start assembling the border of the puzzle with the edge pieces first. The border defines the space I'll be working in and provides me with a frame.

This process can work for boxing too. Start by categorizing what you find by themes and create folders for each theme. Some of the themes I found in Charles's box included family, friends, activism, community, jobs, interests, kitchen, milestones, philanthropy, art, health, and love. Once I sorted my own box into themes, I identified the "edge pieces" (i.e., the main pieces reflected in some pivotal events or stages in my life) that would help me build a timeline in different folders for each theme. That timeline became my framework in which I could start filling the rest of the pieces I had, until I began to see a full picture.

Those I've coached in putting their boxes together had similar yet different approaches to beginning their boxes. Joanne, an independent marketing and advertising consultant, identified nine categories that provided her with a framework for her box. In no particular order, her categories and some of her comments were the following:

1. **Family milestones:** "Unfortunately I don't have much further back than my grandparents, but I will try and collect the relevant information I can from family members and public files."

2. **Relationships:** "I'm referring to people in my life. Some came in and out of my life for a reason, but they had an impact, and they matter."
3. **Education:** "This includes how the world shaped me: Kennedy's assassination, turmoil in the sixties, Vietnam, etc."
4. **Career:** "All about my zigzag path and connecting the dots."
5. **Travel:** "I have been lucky enough to go to incredible places."
6. **Causes:** "Those causes I have been involved in and those I currently support and why."
7. **Cultural events:** "Music, movies, plays. Books that are memorable for significant reasons and silly reasons."
8. **Spirit:** "My relationship with nature or other things that fill my spirit. Events that feel mystical. Color."
9. **Leisure:** "It's all about fun."

When you start reviewing your life, it might feel overwhelming, and it's easy to get lost in the process. My experience with my own box and with coaching others taught me that a good way to start is by creating a basic timeline of your life that includes major events worth remembering. Start the timeline anywhere you want. If creating one timeline for your life seems too difficult or overwhelming, you can consider creating separate timelines for each theme of your life (e.g., family, friends, jobs, trips, hobbies, etc.). Each item listed on your timeline(s) will open up memories and stories to which you will add pictures, mementos, written or recorded anecdotes, or other tangible representations as you continue boxing. You then decide which categories or themes you would like to preserve. The following chapters of this book address some of the common themes of our lives and explore ways to commemorate these in our boxes. Look at the white canvas, sort the pieces, put together the edges, and move forward, bird by bird.

Charles's Life Timeline from My Archaeological Digging

I created a timeline of many of the things I learned about Charles based on the information I found in his box. I offer an abbreviated version to give you an idea of what a Box of Life can tell you about a person. You'll see he was a creative man who was not afraid of trying new things and was always involved in projects. Imagine if you had similar information about each of your ancestors. Imagine if your descendants had similar information about you.

Charles Morris Stern

Charles was born in New York City on April 6, 1920, to Polish parents Louis Stern (a barber) and Dora Wollman.

Charles was the eldest of three siblings. Mortie was the youngest and Helene was the middle child.

During tough times in the 1930s, Charles found a way to earn some extra money for his family. On rainy days he would go down to the Far Rockaway train station and offer rental umbrellas to commuters coming back from work for a small fee, expecting them to return the umbrella the next day at the station.

At the age of fourteen, he set off to make a name for himself in broadcasting. His first stint was with WINS radio station, where Martin Weldon, later executive of WCBS, gave him a start. He began by producing sound effects.

He earned money in high school working in radio and theater.

He was raised Jewish Orthodox, changed to Conservative, and then finally became Reform in 1960.

He attended Far Rockaway High School.

He served in World War II, 241st Coast Artillery, then returned to New York and worked in sales management.

He married Mildred Belle Ring (born in 1916) on July 4, 1948. They were married for sixty-four years.

He and Mildred had one daughter, Ina Gail Stern, born on September 23, 1950.

They lived in Lynbrook, Long Island, New York, where they were members of Temple Israel in Lawrence, New York.

He was a chemical sales manager and consultant for a New York–based company in the 1950s.

He was a cartoonist and an oil painter.

His hat size at one point was 6¾.

He quit smoking in 1965.

In 1971 he moved with his family to San Antonio, Texas, because his wife developed chronic bronchitis and needed a change of climate. There he joined Temple Beth El.

He pursued his love of reading by becoming a sales representative for a firm that published books for teachers about how to teach children to read.

He became a literary agent who represented fifteen authors in securing publishing contracts, among them romance novelist Arlene James, published by Silhouette in 1983. He was the only agent in Southwest Texas, and one of only 250 in the entire country. He sold his first book, Robyn Carr's historical romance *Chelynne*, to Little, Brown and Company in 1978. He was paid 10 percent of sales by the authors for his representation, and he sold five books during his first year as an agent.

He ran for councilman in San Antonio with the campaign slogan, "Vision, direction, and conscience. You do have a choice."

He was a columnist for *Ageless Times* for almost two years, writing about issues affecting senior citizens.

CHARLES M. STERN

At 64 most men are looking forward to retirement. At 64 **Charles M. Stern** is looking forward to involvement. He is a candidate for city councilman, district 9 in the April 6th city election.

Charles Stern is not a rich man. He's a quiet man of inner strength and conviction. He is a business consultant by profession in the areas of public and industrial relations. He has been a construction materials quality control expert. He has served as consultant on some of the biggest construction projects in the country.

Charles Stern is a strong believer in justice. He believes in law and order. He believes we can build a better community through improved educational opportunities. He believes in efficiency in government.

But, perhaps his best qualification is his willingness to listen to people with different points of view. He enjoys good constructive discussion. He says, "It's good for the circulation."

Charles Stern thinks the incumbent city councilman from district 9 has not been responsive to the people. **Charles Stern** will be. **Charles Stern** is a man of action...not words.

Vote for Charles Stern April 6th. This time around, you DO have a choice.

THE MOBILE CAMPAIGN OFFICE WILL VISIT YOUR NEIGHBORHOOD SOON.

Charles's campaign sheet

He directed marketing and PR relations for Cleaning Ideas, a San Antonio–based manufacturer in the mid-1980s.

For twelve years he hosted the *Senior Spotlight* talk show on KKYX AM, a radio program at 6:00 a.m. and 10:00 p.m. on Sundays. The show was discontinued in 1985.

He became the chairman for the Texas Senior Citizens Association Convention in 1993.

He used his marketing acumen to help Colgate Palmolive Corp. set up its first store selling directly to the public in Austin, Texas.

He established and underwrote the Louis and Dorothy Stern Community Service Award in memory of his parents at the San Antonio Jewish Family Services in 1990, awarded to the most active volunteer in the community.

He was a member of B'nai B'rith of San Antonio Brandeis Lodge and copresident in 1994. B'nai B'rith is a Jewish service organization committed to the security and continuity of the Jewish people and the State of Israel and to combating antisemitism and other forms of bigotry.

He hosted the Focus on Living talk show on Catholic Television in San Antonio at 8:00 p.m. the first Monday of each month. Former Mayor Henry Cisneros was his first guest.

He studied the sacred Torah Hebrew letters and sculpted twelve of the twenty-two. He believed he was the first person to do so in almost 3,500 years. He spent 60–120 hours sculpting each one of his letters.

He served on the executive board of the Senior Citizens Council of Bexar County in 1998.

He presented the Hebrew letters he sculpted to the Institute of Texan Cultures in San Antonio, Yeshiva Museum in Manhattan, and the Klutznick Museum in Washington DC, as well as to private collections.

He pursued a new career as a sculptor in his sixties.

He suffered from a coronary artery disease, hypothyroidism, osteoarthritis, and prostate cancer.

He persuaded College Skills Center in Texas to develop a college-based program to train teachers how to teach children to read.

He stopped sculpting when a shoulder injury kept him from raising his arm higher than shoulder level.

He wrote a book about his mother's life.

He acted and directed in the community theater.

He wrote and published two novellas when he was in his eighties. He also taught himself to play the organ.

He presented his own production of *Life Begins at Eighty* at the Robert and Pearl Seymour Center in North Carolina and *Gin and Tonic* by John Clifford at the Reader Theatre in April 2001.

Together with Mildred he traveled to Alaska, Hawaii, the Caribbean, Israel, and other places.

He portrayed Santa Claus in San Antonio television commercials and had public appearances with the "Buppets" in a popular campaign for Via Metropolitan Transit Authority.

In 2002, he and Mildred moved to Chapel Hill in North Carolina to be closer to their daughter.

He was a member of the Durham-Chapel Hill Jewish Federation Board for almost two years.

With his friend, Sol Gordon, he cofounded a program in North Carolina with the goal to build self-esteem in early childhood, especially for children at risk.

He was a motivational speaker who challenged senior citizens with the motto that guided his life: *Having a Project is the secret to longevity.*

In 2005, he reached out to a few editors with a book proposal for *Redefining Your Life after Fifty*, which included ten chapters, each with fifteen questions to help promote realistic decisions for the future. He also pitched a series of books, including *Coping with Aging at Seventy* and *Finding Companionship at Eighty.*

He was proud of his daughter Ina's professional accomplishments and her work at Algonquin Books of Chapel Hill, North Carolina.

He and Mildred contributed $18,000 to establish the Charles M. and Mildred R. Stern Art Education Fund at the Yeshiva University Museum in 2006.

In his nineties he went on a trip to Ireland.

- Create a basic timeline of your life that includes important milestones, defining moments, and major events worth remembering.
- Consider creating different timelines to tell your story (e.g., timelines focusing on friends, jobs, milestones, hobbies, romance, vacations and trips, education, etc.). If you're able, add pictures to the timelines.
- When putting together a Box of Life for someone else, help them create timelines. If necessary, do some detective and archaeological work to fill any gaps.

A Tangible Box or a Digital Folder, or Both?

Your Box of Life can take any shape or form. Some people prefer to place treasured mementos and documents into a physical box. Some will choose a memory board hanging on the wall. Many of us gravitate toward a digital repository. And some opt for a hybrid approach, using a combination of all the above. There are no rules. Use any creative form you can think of. The only rules are that it should be intentionally organized, and it should portray a life story.

By giving me a physical box, Charles made it easy for me to know what he cared about in addition to everything he shared in the conversations we had over the years. He didn't send me off on a detective journey to search every corner of his house or computer, looking for clues and stories. He was an organized fellow in general, but as he started to feel the weight of the years, he immersed himself in his memories and memorabilia, decided which were most important, and consolidated them into one place—his cardboard box.

I asked several people where they kept memories, and most of them shared with me that they have physical boxes, digital files, videos on their cell phones, and a variety of containers and suitcases scattered in different places throughout their homes. I asked them if they were telling the story of their lives through the memories that they kept. Not one of them had thought about that idea before, and they were intrigued by it.

Kayla, a family friend, told me that her stories and box are stored in her heart, but she was concerned they will be forgotten if she does not create a digital file or a physical, tangible box. I'm afraid she is right! She said, "It would be helpful to have an intentional location to help me store all those memories. It would be even more helpful if I knew that in ten years my kids will be looking at them, and that in a hundred years my great-grandchildren will be opening my box and learning about me." If Kayla doesn't act soon, her grandchildren and certainly her great-grandchildren will be in the same situation most of us find ourselves in now. We are either trying to piece our roots together or are coming to a dead end with no answers.

In my case, I've kept many mementos from the various places I've lived, but they were never organized as my life story. The problem I encountered when I started building my box was that my things were scattered all over the place. It took me a few months to go through them. At the time I thought, "I wish I had created my box in one place as I was going through life." Then I went on to think, "How much easier it is these days with the help of technology, where we can upload files, record voices and videos, and get organized as we go."

Juan, an expat who I've been coaching, told me he has a shoebox with family photos and mementos in his closet. He refers to it as "my family history box." The shoebox was passed down by his grandfather to his dad, and then to him. He keeps adding chapters from his own life to that history. Juan shared with me that he is concerned his kids couldn't care less about the shoebox in the closet. "They might even lose it if I give it to them. Their heads are somewhere else," he said. Juan decided to take pictures of the mementos, scan everything in the box, record some family stories, and upload them to the cloud.

Boxing for Our Kids

Laila, a minimalist, mother of five, and retired lawyer, created a digital Box of Life for each of her children. She created and labeled files with the following messages for her kids:

- The day I gave birth to you
- The first time you walked and talked
- Your first birthday party
- A picture of the two of us on your first day of school
- Challenges you've overcome
- Fun times
- Things I've kept for you
- The day you got your first job
- What I've learned from you
- What I always want you to remember about me

My son, now in his late twenties, told me he prefers his box to be digital, taking advantage of the technology available (YouTube, Vimeo, voicemails, texts, social media feeds, Google photos, applications, etc.). He believes that watching people tell their stories on video is of great value. He makes sure to record me and my husband in action during moments that he considers memorable. Many of the clients I'm coaching also prefer a digital box— they're at different stages in life and value the versatility of digital storage.

I like having a tangible box. It is heartwarming for me to touch the paper and enjoy the handwriting of those who preceded me. I enjoy holding the recipes my mother-in-law put together for me and find comfort perusing the letters my best friend wrote to me back when letters were handwritten and mailed in an envelope. I loved holding the yellowed paper on which Mildred wrote Charles Valentine's Day poems. All that said, I also like having a digital box. Digital boxes feel safe in the cloud and are easier to share. They are better for a generation of minimalists and for those who enjoy interactive alternatives.

If you opt for a hybrid box with both a physical and virtual component, don't forget to mention the other in each box so future generations know to look in both places!

Reflect and Take Action

- When seeking all the things that can feed your Box of Life, look inside drawers, closets, and shoeboxes. Search for things in your basement, attic, or in any other places where you've collected memories and mementos. Might you have items in the homes of other family members?
- Most importantly, when looking for memories, search in your heart. Look into your emotions and feelings.
- Interview old friends and family members to find out what items they might have which share relevant stories that include you or your family.

Curate Your Life

Charles's daughter Ina told me that she went through many boxes filled with papers and mementos that belonged to her father. But Charles gave me just *one* box. In that single box, he curated his life story and summarized who Charles Morris Stern was.

Building your box is like embarking on the task of editing the movie of your entire life and limiting the content to no more than a few hours, focusing on the messages you want the audience to take away. The choices you make as you assemble your box are very personal, as they tell your unique story and show future generations what you felt was important to be remembered.

Just like Charles, you must be a strict curator of your Box of Life. If I asked you to tell me your life's story, would you report every single thing you've done every day since the moment you were born? Or would you highlight a few stories, snippets, and facts that represent the core of your identity? The latter is the process I encourage you to take in building your Box of Life. Focus on the stories and mementos that best preserve and summarize who you are. Think about your box not as a public storage unit (a cacophony of random items), but rather a carefully crafted exhibit.

You might be wondering how to distinguish the trivial from the meaningful moments in our lives. Which memories are most important, even if all of them make us who we are as a whole? Charles once told me to choose only the most important items to discuss at a meeting; otherwise, it would be too long and people would lose sight of what we were supposed to accomplish in the first place. My reaction was, "But everything on the agenda is important!" With an edge of frustration in his voice, he responded, "Well Orit, if everything is important, then nothing is." My friend was right. We must distinguish what is *important* from what is *not that important* when putting our Box of Life together.

A Box of Life is fluid and evolving. It changes and grows as we progress through life. As our priorities change, our ideals evolve and our lessons multiply. The Box of Life is a series of snapshots of what is meaningful to us at different stages of our lives. Imagine it as a living, breathing entity—one we must curate over time, at different stages of our lives.

Time Capsule or Box of Life?

There are many different creative ways to box. I love the story of someone who, just like Charles, had never heard of a Box of Life but in some ways created her own. Phyllis was born in Melbourne, Australia, on July 5, 1919, and spent her life in South Africa. Her daughter described her as "a woman ahead of her times—a wife, a mother, a physician, a photographer, an intrepid traveler who visited far-flung places on her own before most people had even heard of those places. She was a quiet intellectual who was an avid reader, a writer, a family historian, a collector, and a forward-thinking dreamer." With that spirit, Phyllis put together a time capsule for her children and grandchildren. She gave her children a box with the following instructions: "Not to be opened till ten years after my death!"

She brought her time capsule to the United States from South Africa on one of her visits in the early '90s. It was stored in her daughter's attic until after she passed away in 2000 and was eventually opened in Washington DC with her then adult grandchildren ten years later. Her daughter shared, "We were so excited, especially me, as I had wanted to break the rule and open it after my mom died, but the kids were horrified and said, 'No, Granny wanted us to wait!' We joked about all the kinds of things that could have been in the box, including gold coins and diamonds! No such luck! But what we found was priceless. Mom included some very interesting newspapers from the '50s, some South African political articles, as well as some personal items of my father's and hers. We were mostly in awe that she had done this and loved the window into what she had thought about. It spurred me to do a similar thing for my kids and grandkids."

Phyllis intended her time capsule to reveal something about her when she was no longer around, just as Charles hoped his box would empower me to let the world know who he was. Phyllis's box included what mattered most to her during different stages of her life; therefore, it was a dynamic time capsule! Her story is another one that

Phyllis's time capsule

reminds us of how universal the impulse to *box* is. The fact that she curated her life in one box and yet accomplished her goal of sharing what mattered most to her is a good example of how less can be more.

Reflect and Take Action

- Save your story as you journey through life. It is a lot easier than deciding one day to look back and try to curate a whole life, much of which by then might be lost, leaving you feeling overwhelmed.
- Curate what you find. Select items that complement each other without much overlap. Choose the most meaningful memories, documents, photos, mementos, etc. that reflect your essence, who you are, and how you live your life. This is an ongoing process.
- The Box of Life is a living collection. It evolves as you move forward in life and shift priorities.

Your Memory Box, Journals, and Ethical Will Belong inside Your Box of Life

Since I've started coaching people in putting their boxes together, many have told me that they already have a memory box, journal, or ethical will and asked how these were different from a Box of Life. For those who are not familiar with an ethical will, it is a nonbinding letter or video that passes ethical and spiritual values, life lessons, advice, and life purpose from one generation to the next. The goal of an ethical will is to link a person to both their family and cultural history. The concept originated as a document in ancient Jewish tradition. In modern times, people of all traditions write ethical wills.

Estate professionals use the ethical will to help their clients articulate values and inform charitable and personal financial decisions. All of these complement each other, but there are key differences. Let's start by comparing memory boxes and journals to a Box of Life.

	Memory Box	Journal	Box of Life
Definition	A box that holds physical items of sentimental value	A written account of our thoughts and feelings	A curated box that holds your most treasured sentimental items and writings that explain the significance of each item or any other aspect of your life's story (such as values, lessons learned, etc.)
Storage	A physical box	A notebook	A physical box or any creative alternative, including virtual spaces
Examples of items stored	First lost tooth, wedding invitation, dried flowers, or photos	A description of our day and insights	A curated variety of mementos that support your story and how you want to be remembered. It can also include your memory box, journals, and ethical will.
Who it may be meaningful to	The owner of the memory box	The owner of the journal and others who know the owner	The owner of the box and generations to come

When putting together a Box of Life, we reflect on our personal experiences, decisions we have made, and what we value most in life. This can be a useful guide for articulating our will or our ethical will. And like our journal and memory box, these also belong in our Box of Life.

———

Imagine we could open Abraham Lincoln's, Albert Einstein's, Muhammad Ali's, or your great-great-grandparent's Box of Life and peek into their true souls, life stories, and lessons learned. Imagine someone could explore your box and get inspired by your life. What would you want them to learn?

> *"Just as an amnesiac who has no memory of his past has lost the sense of who he is, so do we need stories from our past to give us a sense of our own identity."*
> —Vera Rosenbluth

Chapter 3

We All Have Stories to Tell

"To be a person is to have a story to tell."
—**Isak Dinesen**

Everybody loves a good story, and every life has many to share. Even if you think your life is nothing special or nothing compared to the feats of fictional heroes or the adventures in blockbuster movies, you have your own unique perspectives and experiences. Your Box of Life is the place for your best stories—the ones that reveal who you are.

Charles was a talented storyteller, not just in person but also through his box. As soon as I opened his box, a powerful wave of stories splashed over me, bringing his life into vivid color. His stories resonated with me, and I could feel my own stories come alive through his.

Anthropologists remind us that storytelling is central to human existence. People have been telling stories throughout history, and not just for entertainment. We tell stories about our days, experiences, jobs, and family to make sense of what happens to us. Through storytelling we teach and learn. Stories stimulate thinking and provide us with ideas for problem resolution. They also weave communities together and open doors to strangers. When we're exposed to stories about personal experiences and raw emotions, we connect what we hear to our own lives, which builds rapport and increases credibility, resulting in higher community engagement. Stories take us to common ground that allows us to overcome our differences by revealing our similarities with others.

How many stories have you heard or shared in the last 24 hours?

Stories Bring the World to Life

Most of my conversations with Charles would start with him saying, "Let me tell you a story." He'd once read that if we tell someone a story about how to survive, that person is more likely to survive. If we only share facts, that person might not pay as much attention or connect the facts to the danger. He said, "If I told you that last week I walked into that bush, got bitten by a copperhead, endured excruciating pain, and thought I wouldn't make it while I was rushed to the hospital in an ambulance, you would be more likely to remain cautious around that bush, as opposed to if I told you simply that there was a copperhead in that bush. Data by itself doesn't engage as much as data embedded within an emotional context."

Eager to learn more about what Charles told me, I came across Jennifer Aaker, an American behavioral scientist at Stanford University. In her video "Harnessing the Power of Stories," Aaker concluded that people remember information up to twenty-two times more clearly when it is weaved into narratives than when it's presented as facts alone.[1] Immediately, I recalled those college teachers whose lectures were filled with stories and how much more interesting their classes were. I thought of speakers who start with presenting data and then incorporate that data into a story, and how you can clearly see the audience's body language perk up the moment the story begins.

There is no doubt that when we hear or read a well-told story, our brains

---

[1] Jennifer Aaker, "Harnessing the Power of Stories," VMware Women's Leadership Innovation Lab, https://womensleadership.stanford.edu/resources/voice-influence/harnessing-power-stories.

react as if we are experiencing it ourselves. "Let me tell you a story" is what a Box of Life should say every time we open it up.

Reflect and Take Action

- What stories do you want to include in your box? Look into your timeline and jot down notes about three stories you would like to share. They could be funny, happy, or sad-but-meaningful stories from different stages of your life.
- Include those that create an emotional connection. And remember, most times the real story *is* in the details.
- When you look at your life, can you see an overarching story? If you can, briefly describe it. Use no more than five sentences.

The Comfort Found in Our Stories

When I started writing this book, my dad got inspired to collect his stories and put his Box of Life together. His health was declining. Soon after building his box, he fell and was in home hospice for almost ten months before leaving us on July 24, 2021.

These days, I find myself often hugging his box, holding on to his life and memories. I find comfort in knowing that the things that mattered most to him will live on with our family forever.

My good friend Greg, who lost his dad a few years ago, shared with me how much solace he finds in skimming through the pages of his deceased dad's diary. Every page is a story, and through those pages his dad comes back to life. "It feels as if I am there with him, as if those stories were part of my story. Which in many ways, they are," Greg explained.

The comfort found in stories has multiple dimensions. For many, hearing about those who endured trials and survived is inspiring and encouraging.

For others, stories are comforting because they often narrate memorable moments when someone overcame an obstacle, and the story proves that no matter how much challenging our current situation may be, we are able to rise to the occasion and overcome that challenge.

The stories preserved in a Box of Life can help children cope with the loss of a parent, sibling, or grandparent. The contents of the box can be comforting to children who may not understand why someone they cared about left them forever. With that in mind, Tamika, a forty-five-year-old nurse who was recently diagnosed with an aggressive cancer, decided to put together boxes for her two kids, Malik (seven) and Tenaya (four).

Tamika said, "Each box will contain items and stories that represent our family: photos of ourselves with a story behind it, drawings we did together, notes from friends and family, letters from me . . . anything that reminds us of how much we love each other. As time goes on and my kids move forward with their lives, these boxes will be something that they can look back on when they need something familiar or comforting—and it will be something they can go to when they need proof that Mommy, no matter where she is, loves them more than anything! Each story in those boxes will be a story they can share among themselves and with others. They are young and if I don't preserve those stories for them, there will come a time when they won't remember them anymore. I need to know that I'm doing as much as I can for them to find comfort. Their boxes will speak to a clear message. I want my children to always remember

- that they were wanted;
- that they were loved by their mother and father;
- that they have a strong support system within their family and friends;
- that they were special to me, and I loved them more than anything; and
- how much fun we had together—as a family, with friends, and with each other."

Director Mark Travis wrote, "The essentials of life (food, water, air, sleep) pass through us. Nothing remains. We take them in, absorb their essence, and then let them out. Maybe it's the same way with story. We need to create our stories. We need to allow them to grow inside us. We need to feed them knowing they will feed us. And then we need to let them go, to share them. In sharing, every story will generate or stimulate more stories, more nourishment. And life stays in balance."[1] By looking into Charles's and my dad's boxes, their stories grow inside me, they feed me, and they stimulate more stories and more nourishment. That nourishment is comforting. I hope the same holds true for Tamika's children.

Reflect and Take Action

- What three stories of your own or your ancestors' lives bring you comfort?
- Is there a family member whom you could help with their box to ensure that their stories are saved?

"We create stories, and stories create us."
—Chinua Achebe

Stories Are Therapeutic

Life stories promote personal growth for both the narrator and the receiver. They help us make sense of the world, remember the past, and dream for the future. Stories create emotional connections and better understanding of other people's experiences.

---

[1]   Mark Travis, "What Is a Story, and Where Does It Come From?," *The Wrap*, November 9, 2011, https://www.thewrap.com/what-story-and-where-does-it-come-32636/.

But we have to remember that the stories we tell can be positive or negative. There are times when we might find ourselves presenting a dark version of an experience when in fact there were other perspectives.

During coaching sessions, I often ask my clients, "Is there another story you can tell yourself?" This question leads to an *aha* moment when they realize there is more than one narrative about everything. The stories we choose to tell ourselves create the world we live in.

We can carry within ourselves stories that limit us or stories that expand our horizons. Research has shown that telling positive stories about ourselves increases our ability to perform better. We always need to decide what story we want to tell ourselves. I declared Charles the master of knowing how to choose stories that would invite growth and confidence. His box reflected that ability.

As we put together our boxes, we become an observer of our own life, and we have an opportunity to explore our stories and the meaning we have attached to them. As with coaching, putting together or unboxing a Box of Life is not therapy per se, but it is therapeutic.

"Stories have to be told or they die, and when they die, we can't remember who we are or why we're here."
—Sue Monk Kidd

From Clutter to a Story

There is a scene in *The Marvelous Mrs. Maisel*, a Netflix show that cracks me up and makes me cry at the same time, that seems to be an ad created for the Box of Life Project.

Spoiler alert!

Susie learns that her roommate died of a stroke. She is given a box of *stuff* that he left behind; they refer to the box as "his junk." When Susie opens the box, she learns many things she didn't know about her roommate. "This guy lived a life, and I never knew any of this," she laments, fighting back tears. That box that Susie received was clearly her roommate's Box of Life and not his junk. Unfortunately, because it was just a box no one knew about, and it was not attached to any story that others were previously aware of, it could have passed as just clutter to be thrown away. At an emotional funeral ceremony, thanks to his box, loved ones and strangers alike were able to learn about a remarkable life.

Nadav, in his thirties, told me, "My box will be clutter to everyone except me. It's full of things that are significant to me but not to future generations. For example, the coat-check ticket from my wife on our first date . . ." Nadav is right—why would a future generation care about a coat-check ticket? However, if that same coat-check ticket had the accompanying story about the first date in writing or recording, it would take on real significance for future generations who will be able to relate to first dates.

How many old photos do you have where you can't identify the people or the occasion? How much paperwork do you have that you no longer remember why you kept in the first place? How can we make something meaningful to us also important to someone else? The answer is in the stories we attach to them.

Reflect and Take Action

- If there are objects or mementos that you plan to put in your box, include the story behind them. Attach a label or photograph to the object and record or write the story behind it. Make it clear why the item is significant to you.

Charles's Story beyond His Timeline

In Charles's box I found facts that are indisputable—the date of his birth, name of his wife, titles of articles he published. There was plenty of information that revealed a chronological life story—the facts I list in his timeline on page 29. But what fascinated me even more was the subjective information the box revealed. Our lives are not just composed of the events that take place each day. Our lives are what we do with our circumstances and the stories we tell ourselves, which are shaped by our values, beliefs, and attitudes. We all wear a particular set of lenses that colors the way we narrate the same set of events, and there are an infinite number of creative versions.

Let me elaborate by inviting you to try the following exercise:

1. Write a paragraph introducing yourself by only stating facts, things that are indisputably true. Avoid any bias. For example: I was born on January 31, 1967, in Israel. My dad left when I was a newborn to defend Israel in the Six-Day War.
2. Read what you wrote out loud.
3. Proceed to write a new paragraph introducing yourself. This time also state assumptions, things that are not facts but you believe to be true about you. For example: I was a cute baby and the fact that my dad had to leave when I was a newborn was traumatizing for me.
4. Read out loud what you wrote. What do you notice? How are your assumptions influencing your own story? Which story did you feel more comfortable with?

It is important to distinguish between facts and assumptions whenever we share or listen to a story. Both are essential because they each provide information that make up the ultimate story that will be remembered.

Assumptions constitute most of the world we live in. We make deductions about what we see based on our own beliefs, prejudices, and emotions.

Paying attention and distinguishing between assumptions and facts, while appreciating both, is of great importance. If we listen only to our assumptions, it is hard to hear the *true* story; by freeing our narrative of those assumptions, we gain clarity about what really happened. At the same time, recognizing our assumptions helps reveal our values and emotions. The Box of Life hosts both facts and assumptions.

The distinction between the two helps us get grounded in reality. We are constantly telling ourselves stories about everything. We do so by surrounding facts with our beliefs and assumptions. We choose what story to tell, to react to, and to live by. It is important to become aware of what is factual and what is assumed. Only then we can ask ourselves, "Now that I've untangled the facts and assumptions, what other story can I tell that will help me move forward?"

Back to Charles's box: I found many things that led me to create my own assumptions of who Charles Stern was. Even if I had never met Charles, by looking at what he chose to include in his box, I could still share what I believe were his personality traits and values. Charles was inquisitive. He was driven and hard working. He was opinionated, kind, and passionate. Charles was sophisticated. He had a strong dose of *chutzpah*—a Yiddish word for shameless pluck, audacity, and brass. Charles was an avid reader, a gifted storyteller. He was charming, persistent, educated, spiritual. He was an extrovert and greeted every stranger. He was a thinker. He was resourceful and skillful. He had boundless energy to explore the meaning of life, truth, and beauty. He embraced change rather than fearing it. He had a growth mindset. He was an activist. He was creative and artistic. He lived life to the fullest.

The value in Charles's box was in the things I found that described his essence. It was not just chronological facts; it was in the stories and attributes attached to those facts. Anyone going through his box could make different assumptions. Most of the assumptions are debatable according to the individual lenses we are using. Did he really live his life to the fullest? Was he persistent enough? Was he charming to everyone? Was he *happy*—assuming we can agree on a definition of happiness? My personal assumptions lead me to believe the answer is "yes" to all these questions, and I'm thrilled to share more about him through the pages of this book so you can come to your own conclusions.

> "The key to immortality is first living a life
> worth remembering."
> —Unknown, but often accredited to Bruce Lee

Chapter 4

Sifting and Sorting Our Memories

"The power of nostalgia lies not just in honoring the past but in bringing it forward to the present to make our lives richer and more meaningful. It isn't necessarily about wanting to go back."

—Dr. Krystine Batcho

Spanish-born filmmaker Luis Buñuel's memoir stated, ". . . memory is what makes our lives. Life without memory is no life at all . . . Our memory is our coherence, our reason, our feeling, even our action. Without it we are nothing."[1]

Regardless of whether they are good or bad, cherished or feared, memories shared as stories are the heart and core of the Box of Life. All of our most important memories are invited into our boxes, and they create a rich representation of our complex lives. As I sorted through Charles's box, I felt as if I were boarding a one-way flight into the past. His memories triggered my own memories. Learning about his childhood made me think about my own. Over time, I realized I was embarking on a round trip. It was a flight that took off from the present, landed in the past, and then returned to the present. My suitcases were loaded with souvenirs that included life stories,

---

[1]   Luis Buñuel, *My Last Sigh: The Autobiography of Luis Buñuel,* Vintage, March 26, 2013.

lessons, inspiration, and important insights that equipped me with wisdom for the future.

Boxing Memories

My fascination with memory and memories began while pursuing my master's degree as a learning specialist at CAECE University in Buenos Aires, Argentina. I had many questions: Why do some people remember more than others? Why can we remember some things easily, others hazily, and still other things not at all? Why do we sometimes re-create memories rather than remember them as they occurred? Furthermore, how do we know if certain memories are real or if we were just told about them, or maybe saw a photograph or video and then convinced ourselves they were real? As I began writing this book, which extensively covers memories and preserving moments, these questions naturally surfaced.

I decided to unearth my college notes as well as dive into today's most current research. It is important to note that memory is a fascinating, complex, rich topic, and there is still so much that scientists do not understand. In the pages that follow, I only briefly touch on the function of memory that supports the idea that putting together a Box of Life is not just about revisiting the past. Rather, boxing has long-lasting, enriching effects on our present and even future selves.

Our Memory and Our Box of Life Complement and Enrich Each Other

	Memory	Box of Life
What are they and what do they do?	• It is the processes we use to acquire, store, retain, and retrieve information. • It is a deep ocean of images, sounds, sensations, and information that inform us on how to behave. • It allows us to develop a sense of who we are and to understand why our lives look the way they do.	• It gives order and organization to all the information stored in our memory. • As with our memory, when we look into our Box of Life, we develop a sense of who we are, what our lives look like, and why.
How reliable are they?	• Our memory is far from perfect. Divergences can occur between what we internalize as a memory and what actually happened. • With time, memories lose their rich vividness and can also become distorted. • Our brain tends to fill in blanks and inconsistencies by making use of imagination and similarities with other memories. • Memories are also affected by how we internalize events through our perceptions, interpretations, and emotions.	• It provides a database of events we have experienced and their impact on our lives. • We curate our Box of Life by choosing what we want to remember and how we want to be remembered.

	Memory	Box of Life
How reliable are they? (cont.)	• We have a natural tendency, known as mood congruence, to retrieve memories that match our current emotional state. For example, when we're sad we might remember another sad situation.	• It transcends our current moods and can help us take a detour from a trip down "sad memory lane," reminding us instead of other positive memories when we need them the most.
How do we retrieve memories?	• Once memories are stored in our brain, we must recall them for them to be useful. The process of remembering information stored in long-term memory is called memory retrieval. • Retrieval cues are stimuli that trigger memory. These cues can be images, sounds, scents, thoughts, texts, sensations, moods, or anything else related to the memory we are retrieving.	• A Box of Life serves as a rich source of retrieval cues that we choose to keep handy for easy access later. Among the many cues are photographs, journals, stories, documents, brochures, and cards. • When we retrieve memories from our Box of Life, our mood changes. We might feel loved simply by looking at an old note from our grandmother or pride from looking at a document reflecting an accomplishment.

	Memory	Box of Life
How do they serve us?	• Our memory serves as a detective function when using past experiences as a reference for solving current problems, and as a guide for our actions in the present and future. It also serves as an adaptive function by recalling positive personal experiences that can be used to maintain or alter undesirable ones. • The life story we develop based on our memory becomes the way we communicate who we are to others.	• Similar to our memory system, the Box of Life provides us with past experiences as a reference or guide for present-day problems. • It captures our life story by preserving personal events and artifacts. It allows us to become our own observers of how we evolved over time and serves as a rich source for introspection.
Why is it important to remember the past?	• Our memories provide us with a sense of continuity and help create and maintain our individual and collective identities. • We learn from the good, the challenging, and the bad that happened to us individually and collectively.	• A Box of Life preserves our individual, family, and community roots. • As philosopher George Santayana said, "Those who can't remember the past are condemned to repeat it." The Box of Life assures that we will never forget.
How are they different?	• Our memories vanish when we die.	• Our Box of Life transcends our existence.

Fact or Fiction?

Because boxing involves thinking about what's important to us, it naturally involves trips into the past, which raises the issue of the fallibility of memory. There's no question that memory can become distorted with the passage of time. By nature, or perhaps on purpose, some of our memories remain, some disappear, and others transform over time, blending truth with fiction. Usually there is a dense fog shrouding the details, no matter how hard we try to remember. One explanation for this phenomenon is that over time, our memories tend to become less episodic (highly detailed and specific) and more semantic (broad and generalized) as the information is repeatedly retrieved and re-encoded in varying contexts.

Because memories are slightly altered every time we share them, they become reconstructions of reality filtered through our minds, far from accurate snapshots of past events. They become entangled with our assumptions. The stories Charles told me, as well as those I found in his box, were mostly consistent, but I will never be certain if, by sharing them repeatedly, his stories were truly as he remembered them, or if they evolved over time. At the end of the day, it doesn't really matter. Even if there is some fiction in the stories we share, the memories we believe are real end up becoming our reality and define our behaviors and choices.

In my Box of Life, I have included my own versions of childhood stories, regardless of whether my mom agrees with the exact details. I choose to preserve my versions because those are the ones that have shaped me. The same thing happens with my adult children. Oftentimes I hear them share memories of occasions that I remember differently, but I choose to follow their versions instead. Sometimes I chime in with my own recollection, but I present it not as the absolute truth, rather as just another perspective. These conversations become fascinating, teaching us a lot about each other as we contemplate why we all have subconsciously changed the same story. Next time you're with a loved one, I invite you to share common memories and explore the differences in how you remember them. Don't get hung up and worry about who is getting a memory right; the "truth" is in each one, as a memory can easily be a matter of perspective.

You might be asking yourself how to tell if a memory is real before including it in your box. "False" memories tend to not have as much visual imagery or as many details as true memories do. They are also less emotionally intense. But as I said before, the memory that you created is part of who you are and how you behave, and therefore has earned its right to be in your box.

Reflect and Take Action

- If you had a time machine that could take you back to a certain time in your life, where would it be? What is it about that stage of your life that makes you want to go back to it?
- What memories from that time do you want to keep in your box? What do they say about you?

Our Earliest Memories

One of Charles's earliest memories was his feeling of joy while sculpting dogs out of bars of soap in the shower. He described to me the sadness he felt every time one of his soap dogs melted and vanished in the water. While it might sound trivial to some, even a memory like this can teach us about Charles's craftsmanship and his love for dogs. The fact that his brain held on to this memory means it's not so insignificant after all, and it likely played a role in forming his character.

When ninety-one-year-old Nathalie and I began the process of putting her box together, her face lit up when she began to look for a picture from her days as a five-year-old ballerina. "I still remember wearing the little pink costume and sashaying on the stage. We would go out to perform for the Confederate veterans and dance with long chiffon scarves. I'd get out on the stage, forget everything I knew, and just kept moving and twirling those scarves until the music ended," she shared. I could see her traveling back in time and feeling the same emotions she felt on stage, even after eighty-six years.

Nathalie as a ballerina
at age five

Nathalie and me boxing together

Our childhood memories, no matter how trustworthy they are, tend to be among the most cherished because that's the period when we started becoming who we are. Most of us don't remember our first couple years of life, a phenomenon known as *infantile amnesia*. Many factors contribute to infantile amnesia, among them our lack of language and narrative abilities. As we grow up, we learn to encode our experiences into words, which makes it easier to build memories. We tend to have a few vivid and meaningful memories from our preschool years, marking the beginning of our autobiographical memory. Asking others about their first memory always leads to a great conversation, bringing the past into the present in fascinating ways.

Memories that have a lot of emotion attached to them are less likely to fade, and first memories are often based on emotional experiences. Turning an incident into a story with a sequence of events in time and place makes it less likely to be forgotten. Perhaps that's why I think my earliest memory is when Neil Armstrong and Buzz Aldrin landed on the moon in 1969. I was only two years old. I remember sitting on my mom's lap in our home in Costa Rica, watching the landing on our black-and-white TV. I recall the memory in black and white; I can't seem to transform it into color. I recall truly being in awe that a man had landed on what I believed was a piece of an abandoned cloud, one I thought had been accidentally separated from a bigger cloud, which explained why the moon always had a melancholic expression on its face. In any case, my box has a printed copy of a newspaper clipping from that historic and impactful day, and I recorded the memory in an Anecdotes/Memories Notebook I've started keeping.

Most childhood memories come to me in snapshots or feelings; a few I can recount in detail, likely because of the emotions they involved. One of these is of a ceremony when I transitioned from preschool to kindergarten. Standing on a big stage, I received my first official notebook and pen from a fifth grader. My pen rolled onto the floor, and everyone laughed and

Me at age four, wearing a costume I loved that my *savta* (Hebrew for grandmother) sewed for me

exclaimed how cute I was. That day, I developed stage fright that I've never fully recovered from. I didn't want to be "cute" and clumsy; I wanted to be impressive! It sounds frivolous, but for me it was traumatic and has shaped who I've become. I have a picture of that moment in my box and talk more about adversities and how they fit into our boxes in chapter 15.

Navigating Life's Little Stumbles. This captured moment of a first-grade ceremony when a pen fell on stage marks the humble beginning of a journey towards self-assurance, reminding us that even the smallest challenges can shape our path to resilience and growth.

Until I started putting my box together, my memories were stored inside my brain, and they were hard to access in an organized way. As I started writing this section and thinking back on my childhood, one memory triggered another, and I wrote them down in my Anecdotes/Memories Notebook. Now it's your turn to open that drawer filled with childhood memories and allow yourself to flow from one to another.

"Some days I wish I could go back to my childhood. Not to change anything, but to feel a few things twice."
—Unknown

To Get You Thinking

When asking those I coach about their most noteworthy childhood memories, I heard a few recurring answers around the following topics:

- a favorite toy
- vacations
- building forts
- getting in trouble
- playing outside with friends
- Halloween
- the ice cream truck

- the playground
- sleepovers
- grandparents
- birthday celebrations
- one-on-one days with a parent
- pets

Do these trigger any memories for you?

Reflect and Take Action

- What are three of your earliest memories? How can you capture them in your Box of Life?
- Flip through pictures from your childhood. Is there any photo that reminds you of a moment that you believe shaped a current behavior or belief that is worth including in your box?
- Did you have a favorite toy or stuffed animal? Why? Where is it now?
- Keep a physical or digital Anecdotes/Memories Notebook where you can write down memories as they come up—you never know when a memory can be triggered. Include stories of moments that you want to remember either because they had a long-term impact on who you are today or because they are simply too good to be forgotten.

- Most of us don't have vivid memories from before the age of three or four years old, so starting a Box of Life for a newborn is a great way to capture their earliest stories.
- Why not help your child—or any children you are close to— remember special moments? Sit down with them and start sharing your own childhood memories and ask them to tell theirs.

Capture Their Memories and Share Yours

When building boxes for children, it is not just about recording their childhood memories but also what memories are important to us from their childhood. What do we want them to remember when they look back at that stage in their lives? What do we want them to remember about their relationship with us? Ramon, a fifty-two-year-old handyman and the father of a teenager, told me, "The first item I will put into my son's box is a picture of our family in Mexico. My son has never met them in person. I will also include the first drawing he ever made of me holding his hand. The third item I will include is a postcard from our first trip out of town—we went to the beach—and a few anecdotes about that trip. The fourth item is a photo of a soccer game where he scored three goals and got MVP just after I convinced him not to quit the team, to which he felt he was not bringing any value. The fifth item is going to be an old-fashioned flip phone, which he used when he was little to call me whenever he would miss me during my very long days at work."

Memories from Our Adolescence and Young Adulthood

Adolescence and young adulthood are important times in memory encoding because we typically recall a greater number of autobiographical memories from these time periods. Most of us, in our middle age, look back nostalgically to that stage of life. We have more memories of that time than we do of any other time.

Memory researchers have found that the strongest memories we hold come from events that happened to us between the ages of ten and thirty. This tendency to have an increased and enhanced recollection of events that occurred during our adolescence and young adulthood is a phenomenon known as the *reminiscence bump*. Memories from high school, like it or not, stay with us forever.

Memory storage is known to increase during times of change, such as the changes in identity that occur during adolescence. Additionally, life events that occur during the time frame of the reminiscence bump, such as graduation, marriage, or the birth of a child, are novel and therefore render them more memorable. Memories found within the reminiscence bump significantly contribute to our life goals, self-theories, attitudes, and beliefs. Thus, the teenage and young adult years are a great time to start putting together a Box of Life.

In Charles's box I found a few things that went back to his teenage and young adult years, including information about his dad's expectations of him, his first job and initiatives, and the story of how he met his wife. There was one memory he told me about which vividly transported me directly to the scene. It was about renting umbrellas at the Far Rockaway train station as a teenager. He described the rain, the sound of the train, and the tired commuters arriving after a long day of work. He'd rent umbrellas to those without one with the expectation that they'd return them at the station the next morning. Charles recognized the memory as revealing the budding entrepreneur in him, along with his willingness to take risks.

My friend Sandra told me that her box contains a lot of memories from adolescence and young adulthood. "It was a very important time for me socially and personally. My teenage friends are to this day the friends I'm most comfortable with. During those years I lost my dad, graduated from college, had a few romantic encounters, got married, and became a mom. For my box I've selected letters, faxes, cards from friends, pictures with stories of how we shared our time together, diplomas and accomplishments, journal entries, poems, pictures, and memorabilia from my wedding and pregnancies."

Interestingly, the one thing that usually lasts forever is the feeling that teenage and young adult memories evoke. I can't remember everything I used to do with my best friends during high school, but I can assure you that Sandra, Natalia, Gaby, Miguel (RIP), and Héctor always made me feel happy and loved.

Reflect and Take Action

- What three memories can you recall from your adolescence and young adulthood that have an impact on the person you are today?
- Reach out to people you know from that time and go down memory lane together to see what memories are triggered that might be worth capturing.
- Ask yourself and others what you miss most about being a teenager and how you can replicate that in your current stage of life.
- Is there a teenager or young adult in your life whom you can invite to start boxing? Are there ways you can contribute or help them start the process?

Midlife Memories

During our midlife, we often find ourselves reflecting on our lives. The first half of our life is often spent learning and working to establish ourselves in the world. The second half is all about taking stock of where we are, what we've learned, and how to make the most of the rest of our life.

Midlife is also a time in our lives in which we are busy living. It is a daily blur of working, grocery shopping, raising our kids, supporting our aging parents, making dinner, walking the dogs, paying bills, planning family outings—the list goes on and on. Our attention is in a hundred places at once, and it's hard to remember everything. I constantly forget the place I set my reader glasses or keys, which one of my 101 passwords is for what, the name of the last book I read, why I set the alarm . . . what was I trying to remember? I laugh about this with friends who are in the same stage of life. (I prefer laughing over crying.)

I felt much better about my memory decline when my physician explained to me that it is more about a change in focus than it is about aging. He kindly said, "Orit, your mind is in too many places at the same time, so don't blame it on aging." But then he added, "Also keep in mind that general fogginess and mild memory lapses are common before entering menopause, as your body is making less estrogen. This is most likely temporary, and your memory will come back to where it was."

If you are in your midlife, you've probably already made some memories that will stay with you forever—but what else do you want to accomplish? What else do you want to experience? How can you use this time to give yourself some peace of mind about where your life is headed?

My midlife is marked by the loss of loved ones, along with several events that make me question my life's direction. For the first time I realized I'm no longer young; people have started calling me "ma'am" or "señora." It is the stage when I officially became an empty nester and miss both my kids deeply. It's also a time when small things begin to make me happy—the way my dog comes to cuddle with me when she knows I need her. Or how my mom still remembers my favorite foods and brings them over on Fridays. Or when my husband brings me sunflowers, which he knows are my favorite, and we can enjoy many fun things that were out of our reach before. During this time, I've added new, lasting friendships, built our first home, and most important, written my first book!

This stage in life for many is a time of accomplishments. Some of us may finally feel comfortable in our own skin and have a sense of pride about what we do professionally. Some of us are still raising kids while others are planning their kids' weddings. Many of us are questioning how we want to live the next half of our lives. It is also a time of routine; we keep going and we keep doing similar things. We might not experience novelty as often as we did before, but we are still creating important memories and gaining insights worth boxing.

I asked my sister-in-law Dalia, a sociologist who lives in Argentina, for her take on visiting the past. She has four daughters whose ages range from elementary school to young adulthood.. Her answer was philosophical and poetic. Dalia wrote, "I'm not one of those people who remembers everything in full detail. My memories present to me as thick brush strokes, in different stages or layers. My past is often linked to the growing up of my daughters, and in their growth, I project mine. My memories don't burn, but they feel very warm and close to me—that said, at times they also seem to want to escape."

Reflect and Take Action

- Even if midlife feels like a bit of a blur, there are no doubt moments that stand out. What are these moments? Why are they special?
- What accomplishments are you proud of? How can you best commemorate them in your box?

- If you're a parent, sometimes it's hard to distinguish between your kids' and your own milestones. Take a moment to tease these apart. What happened in times when you felt most fulfilled as a parent?
- If you are past midlife, what do you remember from that stage that you want to box? How do you feel about those memories now?
- If you're boxing for a parent, ask them about the decades between their thirties and seventies. What stands out? What might they have done differently?

Looking Backward in Order to Look Forward

Danish theologian Søren Kierkegaard, considered the first existentialist philosopher, once said, "Life can only be understood backwards, but it must be lived forwards." I can't agree more.

The Box of Life is a receiver of memories and serves as a backup to our forgetful and selective memory. Although memories spring from the past, they serve us in the present and the future.

Memories influence how we go about living our lives. To understand who we are today, we need to know who we have been. This in turn can inform us about who we want to become and how to get there. We use what we learned from the past to improve the present and build a better future.

When looking at our circumstances not in isolation but as a chain of continuity, we gain new meaning, perspective, and dimension in our lives. English writer Virginia Woolf wrote, "For the present when backed by the past is a thousand times deeper than the present when it presses so close that you can feel nothing else."[1]

One of the first scientific indications that remembering the past and

---

[1] Virginia Woolf, *Moments of Being: A Collection of Autobiographical Writing*, edited by Jeanne Schulkind, Mariner Books, August 23, 1985.

imagining the future are related comes from patients who suffered from amnesia or some degree of memory loss. These patients also lost an ability to see their future or had different ambitions and hopes than prior to the event that caused their loss of memory. In losing memories they also lost a connection to who they fundamentally were, or similarly, who they could become. This happens because many of the same brain structures are used in both remembering and forecasting.

Julie Beck, a senior editor at *The Atlantic*, explains that "humans predict what the future will be like by using their memories. This is how things you do over and over again become routine. For example, you know generally what your day will be like at the office tomorrow based on what your day at the office was like today and all the other days you spent there. But memory also helps people predict what it will be like to do things they haven't done before."[1]

Our Box of Life allows us to bring the past and the future into the present, no matter what stage of life we are at. We can memorialize the present, look into the past with the eyes of today, and plan for the future based on where we are now. I find wisdom in the words of St. Augustine: "Perhaps it might be said rightly that there are three times: a time present of things past; a time present of things present; and a time present of things future. For these three coexist somehow in the soul, for otherwise I could not see them. The time present of things past is memory; the time present of things present is direct experience; the time present of things future is expectation."[2] Our present is constantly moving into the past, and much of our lives are made up of memories of the past and hopes for the future.

It is important to note that as useful as memories are to enrich our present and future, it is healthy to live in the present as much as we can. We need to use the past as a teacher but not as a place to dwell in forever. One of the

---

[1]   Julie Beck, "Imagining the Future Is Just Another Form of Memory," *The Atlantic*, October 17, 2017, https://www.theatlantic.com/science/archive/2017/10/imagining-the-future-is-just-another-form-of-memory/542832/.

[2]   St. Augustine, *Confessions*, book 11, chapter 20, heading 26.

most powerful quotes I have heard, from an anonymous source, reads, "We can't let our present be ruined by a past that has no future."

Living in the past can be an invitation for feelings of regret, grievance, guilt, bitterness, and lack of forgiveness. Similar problems can arise from living in the future. It may be an invitation for feelings of stress, anxiety, tension, fear, and worry. However, recalling the past while living in the present makes way for new perspectives and a sense of accomplishment and survival. The future seen while living in the present inspires a sense of hope and courage.

Reflect and Take Action

- Choose three memories to memorialize in your box. How would you go about choosing them? Examples might include a wonderful highlight, a challenging moment of adversity, or a story that shaped your present self.
- Write a letter or record an audio clip or video to your future self of five to ten years from now. What do you hope for yourself? What do you want your future self to remember?

Life Review Therapy

While doing research on reminiscence and recollection of the past, I had an *aha* moment when I came across the concept of life review therapy (LRT). Patients, mainly in their later stages in life, are invited to recollect and evaluate positive and negative memories with the goal of enhancing mental health and well-being. Personal stories of endurance, joy, sorrow, and recovery help people alleviate sadness, reconnect with achievements, and disperse current negative thoughts. LRT is beneficial to those with dementia or Alzheimer's disease, as it stimulates memories and facilitates forgotten words. It can also help people who suffer from anxiety or depression. When we reflect and speak about certain past experiences, we can relive meaningful moments and tap into the same emotions we felt at the time.

I suddenly realized that I had been not only Charles's friend but also his unconventional, informal therapist and coach during the review of his life. I suspect Charles intuitively knew about my unspoken role as his "life review coach," considering his well-developed intuition that guided him to achieve what he needed to at every point in time. Our conversations brought meaning to his life—I could sense the comfort and acceptance that each story generated and the pride he was feeling in passing his wisdom on.

No matter what life stage we are in, embarking on the process of putting together a Box of Life produces effects similar to those of an LRT session, in which patients recall memories from the past that can help with feelings connected to the present. We reexperience the past when we intentionally remember it. That's certainly what happened to my dad when he started putting together his Box of Life as an eighty-eight-year-old struggling with Parkinson's. He had a spark on his face during the process, in which he took his time. At one point he said to me, "I realized that I had an interesting life and I've accomplished many things. I had just forgotten about them until now. I also had to confront very difficult challenges at times, but I always had the support I needed from my family to keep going."

My *aba* (which means father in Hebrew) spent weeks immersed in the past, looking in every corner of his house, through his drawers, files, photo albums, notebooks, and shoe boxes filled with brochures and other memorabilia. He was searching for all the information about his past that he could find. At the end he gave me an old shoebox filled with documents representing his accomplishments: newspaper clips, correspondence, photos, and much more. It included a letter he wrote to his business stakeholders sharing difficult news about his business that I'd never known about. To my surprise, I found a poem I wrote for him when I was twelve after his dad passed away. He also kept a letter I wrote to him during my teenage years, pleading for privileges and reminding him that I wasn't a child anymore and needed to feel trusted to make the right choices. I had forgotten that I had ever written either of these, and I never knew they meant so much to him.

More often than not, it's only when someone we love is suffering from an illness or has already passed away that we start thinking about all the stories that will disappear with them. Why wait? I'm thankful that I asked my dad to put together his Box of Life. The fact that it was an affirming experience for him, and that I can hug and look at his box now that he is gone, is deeply gratifying.

With my *aba* in our house in Ramat Ha Sharon, Israel. This was a picture found in his box—a picture that speaks to his presence in my life!

During one of the services to commemorate my dad's life after he passed away, I opened his Box of Life and shared the contents with friends and family. By doing so, I brought to light what mattered most to him. As I was sharing, I discovered things I didn't see before, including a photograph of my dad with his classmates in elementary school. It was hard to determine which one of those young boys was him. My husband pointed at one boy and said he thought he found him. As he looked more closely, he noticed that it was marked with an

X. My dad knew that one day we might struggle to identify him. (Follow my dad's lead and always mark yourself in pictures from your childhood or write

My dad working on his Box of Life

a note on the back describing which person you are, along with the date!) Opening his box and going through his life review was therapeutic for me—a comforting reminder that he had a full, well-lived life. If there is one thing I regret, it's not interviewing my dad when he was younger and recording those interviews. If you still have the possibility of doing that with your parents or another elderly relative, don't wait until it's too late.

My mom also went through the exercise of putting her Box of Life together. Interestingly, when she started her box, she focused on others, as opposed to herself. She included pictures of my wedding, my kids' first lost teeth, their school artwork . . . She created a nice story about the people she treasured. But it was an incomplete picture. I had to remind her about her own career as a professional artist and art teacher. Together we went down memory lane to revisit her successful exhibits and her art classes that were always sold out. We also focused on her culinary skills and the delicious, unique dishes she prepared, her friends and extended family, her many trips to exotic places, and so many other things that she had cast off to a distant corner of her mind. As we were sharing these experiences,

Posing next to my dad and my mom, whose artistic name is Shoshana Aviram, during her art exhibit in Bogotá, Colombia

she began to light up with excitement and became inspired about the things she could start doing again at the age of eighty-five.

Boxing with or for Our Parents

When you're trying to preserve memories for your parents, it can be hard to know where to start. You want to create something that will help them remember the good times in their lives and their resilience during those that were challenging. So what do you include in your parents' Box of Life? You could perhaps put together a scrapbook or photo album of times you spent together as a family. Or you might create an online gallery where photos are organized by year or event (e.g., "1986" or "Christmas Eve, 1987"). Another possibility is to create an audio recording of stories about different events throughout your life with your parents.

Think about the things that are most important to your parents—for example, their children, grandchildren, and other family members, their careers, their hobbies, or the places they've visited. Find ways to honor those things by including items and stories that represent them. Remember that the point of creating a Box of Life is to preserve memories for your parents—not just any memories, but those that mean the most to them.

The best way to do this is by asking them questions, such as the following: What are some of the things you dreamed of doing when you were young? What were your favorite childhood books? What music did you love? What places hold special meaning for you? Among all the hobbies and activities you engaged in, which have been the most important to you? How do you want your life stories to be remembered? These questions will help you determine what kind of memorabilia would be meaningful for them—and will also give you greater insight into who they are as human beings outside of being just "Mom" or "Dad."

James, an entrepreneur, decided to create a Box of Life for his parents. His mother was diagnosed with Alzheimer's disease. James shared, "I want my parents to know that their lives have mattered and that their work and sacrifice have made this world a better place for future generations. I want them to know that even though our time together on this earth is limited, the impact of their lives will last forever. I also want them to know that even if they don't remember these things themselves, someone else will be there to remind them—someone who loves them dearly and wants nothing more than for them to be remembered for who they truly are: kind-hearted beings whose presence in this world helped shape it into something better than it was before they arrived. I'm including in their box a note from me thanking them for everything they've done for me, from the most obvious things to those that had an impact on my life without them even noticing that what they did was special."

In my experience, most older adults find recalling the past and putting their boxes together invigorating and empowering. Going down memory lane provides them with a reminder of the meaningful things in their lives. I highly recommend boxing with your parents or elderly friends and relatives. It will facilitate important conversations, solve mysteries, and allow them to travel back to times of glory and times of pain. It might become a rewarding journey of discovery for everyone.

Life Review Is Not Just for the Elderly

Neha, a student at the University of North Carolina, recently shared with me the following: "I believe legacy and life review are important not only at the end of life but also at the beginning and throughout your entire life. It helps you reflect and learn about yourself at every point throughout your journey. I think in this age, where we can constantly dump all our thoughts, pictures, and ideas, and are bombarded by social media, having a tangible space that we can look back and reflect on in our lives is very important." I know many reflective young adults like Neha who are embracing the process of looking back in order to move forward, and who are inspired by their past accomplishments even in moments of self-doubt.

Reflect and Take Action

- What older adult can you invite to put a Box of Life together with? How might you help them with the project? What do you want to know about that person?

Nostalgia

Colombian author Gabriel García Márquez said, "We grow up with dreams in our eyes and songs on our lips and we discover that life is not what we thought it would be. And then, we discover nostalgia." Nostalgia is a natural tendency associated with sentimentality and a yearning for the past, typically for a period or place with happy associations. Nostalgia can be triggered at any time—you might hear a melody, see a face or an object, smell a scent, or even experience certain weather that can bring on a feeling of nostalgia.

The Box of Life is an open invitation for a nostalgic trip.

When I once asked Charles, who often referred to the "good old days," whether he was aware that he was nostalgic to an extreme, he replied, "I live always looking forward to the next thing, and at the same time nostalgia serves me well when I reminisce on old times. I feel better about myself, where I am today, and I get renewed hope for the future." Nostalgic memories come as a reminder that if we once had meaningful experiences and moments, there can be more of them, and the Box of Life plays the same role.

Feeling nostalgic is not only common in elderly people who are looking back and reevaluating their lives but also in young adults who are coping with major life transitions as they leave home for college, get married, or start a new job. Several studies indicate that children as young as seven can experience nostalgia.

Nostalgia's definition has evolved over time. For centuries it was considered a debilitating disorder expressing extreme homesickness (and even now it can be confused with melancholy), but the scientific community's current view has demonstrated that nostalgia has significant benefits for mental health.

Nostalgia's Benefits and The Box of Life

	Nostalgia	The Box of Life
They help us reconnect with meaningful memories.	• Nostalgia helps us connect our past experiences to our present circumstances and derive a greater meaning from our lives.	• The memories in our box remind us that our past holds vital keys and clues to pursuing a meaningful future.

	Nostalgia	The Box of Life
They help improve our moods.	• Sadness, low self-esteem, and meaninglessness are all triggers for nostalgia, but as we engage in nostalgia, it counters these negative states. • Nostalgia helps us regulate distress and boosts our moods. • During uncertain times, being nostalgic can remind us of challenges we overcame in the past and memories that now bring us comfort and joy.	• Looking back at our lives and remembering what else there is beyond our current situation can be a healing and motivating experience. Our box helps us restore the sense that life is worth living, even with all its adversities and challenging aspects.
They promote social connectedness.	• Most of our nostalgic memories tend to focus on positive emotions and social memories that involve intimate relationships, especially with family. Nostalgia can increase our perception of social support and counteract loneliness, boredom, and anxiety.	• In our box we cherish experiences we had with family and friends, such as vacations, celebrations, milestone events, and holidays. We come closer to others when we share nostalgic memories that are stored in our box.

	Nostalgia	The Box of Life
They help us navigate through transitions.	• In times of change, reflecting on the past may help us maintain and adjust our identity. Nostalgia helps us deal with transitions by recalling that there are things that we can still appreciate, regardless of the uncertainty we are experiencing.	• Our box reminds us of other transitions that we have coped with, the people who are still our anchors, and that we have a solid foundation that is stronger than anything else.
They bring warmth.	• Nostalgia makes us feel warmer. That's a fact on a spiritual level and on a physical level! Nostalgic feelings are more common on cold days in which nostalgia modulates the interceptive feeling of temperature through "heartwarming" memories.	• Our box is a source of warmth. Whatever we decide to store in our boxes are reminders of what matters most to us. These are things that brew good feelings from the past to the present and help us spring forward toward a brighter future. They're a hug for the soul!

"I wish there was a way to know you're in the good old days
before you've actually left them."
—Greg Daniels (spoken by Andy Bernard, a character in the
NBC television series The Office)

	Nostalgia	The Box of Life
They provide hope for the future.	• Nostalgia is a past-focused experience with a future-oriented nature. We reference our nostalgic past to remind ourselves what it felt like back then, which in turn promotes healthy, future-oriented behavior.	• Our box serves as a multivitamin for the soul that provides us with all the nutrients we need—wisdom, motivation, and hope—to plan and pursue our future.
They conjure up youthful feelings.	• Nostalgia makes us feel youthful by transporting us to past experiences that generate these feelings.	• Our box captures memories and experiences of the past that energize us every time we revisit them.
They embrace continuity.	• When young adults read the nostalgic narratives of older adults, they also experience nostalgia and connection. Nostalgia prompts us to preserve our cultural heritage. It simultaneously reminds us that we have roots and there is continuity.	• The Box of Life is at the forefront of preserving our cultural heritage.

I consider myself a nostalgia aficionado. I'm sure Charles sensed that, and it became another key factor in our friendship. Being nostalgic provides me with direction and reminders of what's important to me. That said, it's important to remember that living in the past can become a problem if it interferes with living in the present or with planning for the future. It is only good to visit the past so it can become a resource that provides meaning for our present and focus for our future.

Reflect and Take Action

- Are you nostalgic? If you are, what triggers your nostalgia?
- What are the benefits you enjoy from being nostalgic? What are the downsides?
- What ten objects or stories can you include in your Box of Life that will trigger good or comforting feelings when you look at them?

"It Was Better Back Then"

I found an article by Charles in his box that had been published in 1999 in *Ageless Times*, a monthly newspaper for people aged fifty-five and older in Texas. In it he reminisced, "I remember when a neighborhood was a close and caring community. The doors weren't locked, and you could safely walk home any hour of the night without fear. There were no gated communities that locked people away from the realities of life. Sunday was a day of rest and a time for meeting with family, friends, and neighbors. The family was a close-knit group that shared time and trouble . . ."

We often recall the past with rose-colored glasses that make it seem much better than the present. An article I read years ago explained this, suggesting that in the present, we tend to focus on the negative experiences because of survival instinct. We are always on the lookout for threats. Since we do not need to have the same survival instinct when thinking of the past, positive memories are more likely to be remembered. The past always seems to be simpler.

Once, when Charles vented about how much better the world used to be, I asked him to share what exactly was better back then. He paused for a while, which was not common for him, set his eyes to the horizon as if he were looking through time, and said, "Orit, I think the only thing that was better was the fact that I was young." He chuckled, adding, "But as you are asking me about concrete things, I have to admit that we might actually be in a better place right now."

"How so?" I asked.

He replied, "We have less malnutrition, better health care, more advocacy for human rights, less extreme poverty, fewer wars, an increase in life expectancy, plummeting child mortality rates, an increase in awareness about what's right and wrong, an increased awareness on how to take care of our temple (the earth), and the list goes on. We still have a lot of work to do, and certainly our mission to keep getting better is far from over. But overall, Orit, we are heading in the right direction compared to where we are coming from. We just need to maintain our manners and take the time to slow down and look each other in the eyes." I remember this conversation so vividly because it had such a big impact on me.

Charles believed that many aspects of life were "better" in the past, but at the same time he embraced change. Although he missed his youth, he adapted by embracing the idea that "life begins at eighty" (more about that and his life philosophy in chapter 5).

Our general conviction that "things aren't what they used to be" is known as the psychological bias of *declinism*. When we look back on events from our past, we are likely to remember that many things were awesome and almost perfect. As we grow up and experience more life, it takes so much more to be truly awed. We then mistakenly decide that things were better back then. The way we remember (and yearn for) the past is generally distorted and idealized. Being aware of declinism can potentially help us remember that when we think fondly of the past, we are very likely romanticizing our memories. As Franklin Pierce Adams once said, "Nothing is more responsible for the good old days than a bad memory."

But the truth is that declinism is not *all* wrong. Progress always goes hand in hand with loss. Isn't that what evolution is all about? Many of the things older people mourn from their youth don't exist anymore. Even for young adults, there are things from their childhood that no longer exist. As our lives evolve, some things change for the better and some for the worse, but we fall into loss aversion and wind up paying much more attention to what we've lost and thinking life is getting worse. But we don't have to fall into this trap.

Reflect and Take Action

- Do you look at your past through rose-colored glasses? If so, which parts do you romanticize?
- Create a list of five things that you miss from the past that don't exist anymore or have evolved into something different. This will also spark a fun conversation to have with people your age as you go back in time together.
- Name three positive experiences in your life that you at first interpreted as problematic, and three problematic experiences that you at first interpreted as positive.

"The past is in your head. The future is in your hands."
—Unknown

Chapter 5

Values, Life Purpose, and Philosophy

"Your beliefs become your thoughts.
Your thoughts become your words.
Your words become your actions.
Your actions become your habits.
Your habits become your values.
Your values become your destiny."

—Mahatma Gandhi

Values are the beliefs that each one of us consider most important to ourselves and possibly for humanity. Our values speak to who we are. Like our genes, they define us. Like our heartbeat, they keep us going. Together, they act as an internal compass that guides everything from our decision-making to our code of conduct.

What we decide to include in our Box of Life should reveal our values. At the same time, our values should inform what we decide to put in our box. When someone looks at the totality of the things we've decided to keep, they should come to know what we cared about, what kind of person we were, and how we lived our lives.

Are you aware of your core values? Can you articulate them? Do you ever revisit or reflect on them? For most people, the answer to these questions is no. As a result, people go through life blindly, leaving their chance for fulfillment in the hands of fate. Living without awareness of our values is like traveling without a compass or a map and hoping we will reach our destination.

Articulating our values saves us from the risk of getting lost and living a life dictated by what *others* say is best for us. Walking in someone else's shoes is almost never as comfortable as walking in our own. We need to define our values *ourselves* and then live by them. As Canadian-American self-development author Brian Tracy wrote, "Just as your car runs more smoothly and requires less energy to go faster and farther when the wheels are in perfect alignment, you perform better when your thoughts, feelings, emotions, goals, and values are in balance."[1]

Living a life untrue to who we are can lead to internal tension, frustration, anxiety, and even depression. When I hear my clients say vague, instinctual phrases such as "Something's not working" or "It doesn't feel right," it's usually due to a misalignment of their values and their lifestyle. Luckily, through value-based coaching we can take an abstract phrase— "Something's not working"—and turn it into an actionable ambition with solutions that might include creating new habits, adjusting circumstances, or changing choices.

It is only when our lifestyle is aligned with our values that we can truly become fulfilled. When in doubt, refer to your values; they can serve as your guiding compass. They can help you decide which way to go and help determine if you're going in the right direction.

Charles's Values 101

While digging through Charles's box, I found it fascinating to decipher his values based on the items he chose to include. I identified them by looking at his primary roles and activities, the charities he cared about, the way he

---

1   Brian Tracy, *Focal Point: A Proven System to Simplify Your Life, Double Your Productivity, and Achieve All Your Goals*, AMACOM, October 1, 2004.

addressed others, and his personal interests. I was gratified to discover that the values that emerged from my exploration aligned with the person I had come to know throughout our friendship. Some of the core values I found were *connection, being a mensch, open-mindedness, creativity, community, passion, and giving back.* One of these values, being a mensch—the Yiddish word for being a person of integrity and honor—was something Charles emphasized frequently.

In my conversations with Charles and while looking into his box, I found many powerful sentiments and sayings in relation to his values that resonated with me, including the following:

- **Connection:** I found articles in which he wrote about the importance of human connection. Charles used to say, "Always look into people beyond their shell." I take it as a personal mission to break through shells. If I interact with a stranger who seems to be lost in their own world, such as a cranky cashier or a rushed restaurant server, I try my absolute hardest to break through their shell and connect with them. If I can get a smile, my day is made. Part of breaking through this shell is accepting that every individual speaks a unique language based on their culture, beliefs, emotions, and circumstances. Opening your mind and doing your best to understand and speak *their* language will empower you to look beyond their shell.

- **Being a mensch:** Charles believed that respect is not something you can demand. You earn respect by being kind and respectful to others. I believe this too. Even if someone is rude, insensitive, or thoughtless toward me, I don't need to reciprocate that same energy. By remaining kind, I can strip away any power attached to the other person's rudeness or aggression. Without this power, they may realize they should try other behaviors, like being kind, to achieve what they want.

When we act with kindness in response to rudeness, we are refusing disrespectful treatment. We can still maintain our boundaries without emulating the bad behavior of someone else. When Charles witnessed someone being rude, he said, "The first assumption I make when someone is acting poorly is that they are having a bad day or that they didn't learn how to do better." I adhere to his thinking.

- **Open-mindedness:** "Someone else doesn't need to be wrong for you to be right." I always understood Charles when he made this statement. I personally stand in the center for most issues. The center allows me to look to my right and my left and appreciate the issues and wisdom of both sides to make an educated decision. Every issue has many layers and truths to it. I'm a big fan of the book by Douglas Stone, Bruce Patton, and Sheila Heen, titled *Difficult Conversations: How to Discuss What Matters Most*. In it the authors invite readers to engage in *learning conversations* instead of *battle conversations*. In a learning conversation, both sides learn and win. In a battle conversation, there is always a loser. You can still make your point and defend your case in a learning conversation, but you do it in a way that both sides feel enriched by the end of the conversation. *Difficult Conversations* is in my Box of Life's list of books that had an impact on how I act.

- **Creativity:** Charles used to say, "Creativity is my philosophy of life." In his box I found a column he wrote that included the following: "How often do you observe people who seem to remain perpetually young? Don't be quick to believe that it is only attributed to genes, diet, vitamins, or exercise without considering the power of your mind. An active and creative mind can make a huge difference in your ability to stay young and live longer." He goes on to invite the readers to be creative, writing, "You can choose to do anything you want to do, even if you don't do it perfectly . . . Selecting a challenge and meeting it creates a sense of self-empowerment that becomes the basis for further successful challenges." I believe that we're all creative in our own way, and that by tapping into our creativity we can solve almost any problem, create new opportunities, and bring magic to life.

- **Community:** When Charles moved to Durham, he stopped by the local Jewish Federation to say hello, and that was the beginning of creating a new community for himself. We can all find community wherever we are. And no matter how strange or foreign the place, community can make it feel like home. "There is always a community waiting for you, a place where you belong," my mom used to tell me every time we packed up to move to our next destination. I grew up in seven different countries. Every time I moved, the people of the Jewish community in our new home would host us for dinner the Friday of the week we arrived. These dinners were just the beginning of creating a sense of belonging that I am grateful for to this day.

- **Passion:** If Charles had an idea, it would never go to waste. When he was passionate about a topic, he would act on it. Charles believed he was on a mission to inspire others to live their best lives, so why not have a television program about it? I found a script in his box from a monthly TV talk show called *Focus on Living*, which he anchored in San Antonio in 2001. He interviewed guests—therapists, clergy, authors, politicians—about insights on living a better life and then opened the phone lines so listeners could ask questions. Whenever Charles saw a spark, he would ignite it, turning it into a fire and acting on his interests. Sometimes the fire would burn out very quickly, but at least he gave it a shot.

- **Giving back:** Charles lived his life giving his very best to others. As he shared in an interview clipping I found in his box, "One of the pleasures in life is being able to contribute part of ourselves to benefit the society in which we live. If you have a gift of creativity, that's a gift you can give." I also found in his box some writing about a question that Charles loved to talk about: "What is the difference between being wealthy and being rich?" His answer: "Wealth is money; if you have a lot of money, you are wealthy. If in your life you have done all the things that you have planned to do, if you have helped the community, if you have helped other people, if you have contributed your time, effort, and used your talents, if you have made the difference . . . then you are rich. The big question, then, is, Are you wealthy or are you rich? You can have all the money in the world and be poor, and yet you can have a modest income and be rich." To Charles, being rich meant living a life aligned with his value of being a mensch.

This last value reminds me of one of the most touching moments I've experienced in my life. The story is safely stored in my Box of Life. Just after category 5 Hurricane Katrina devastated New Orleans in 2005, the Durham-Chapel Hill Jewish Federation, where I was executive director, started to collect funds to assist the many people who were impacted. A homeless person walked into our office with a five-dollar bill to contribute to our efforts. Those five dollars were worth more than any other contribution we ever received. They reminded us that we can all give back.

Identifying Your Values

To identify your core values, start by reflecting on times when you felt most fulfilled. What contributed to these feelings of fulfillment? What were you doing? Who were you with?

Also reflect on times in your life that included conflict or a sense of uneasiness. Those were most likely times in which you were out of alignment with your core values.

If you are working on identifying your core values, or if you want to review them, you might find the following questions helpful:

- What is truly important to me in life?
- What brings me joy?
- What motivates me every day to wake up and start my day?
- What does *accomplishment* mean to me?
- What would I stand and fight for?
- What have I gone out of my way to do?
- What are some culminating experiences or meaningful moments that I'm proud of?
- If time and money were unlimited, what would I do?
- What's my favorite activity?
- Who inspires me? Why?
- Which charities, if any, do I contribute to and why?
- What would others deem as my strengths and virtues?
- In which organizations have I actively participated? What drew me to these?

Once you've had a chance to reflect on these questions, see if any recurring themes emerge. For example, you might see that it's important to you to be loyal to those you care about. Or you might realize that you believe hard work is a key to success and satisfaction. Jot down any words that tie your experiences together. When I did this exercise, I discovered that I'm at my best when surrounded by people who inspire me with their resilience and positive outlook on life.

I reevaluate my own values every few years. Life events or even just the passing of time can change our values, but more often than not, they remain relatively stable. After all, your anatomy doesn't change overnight.

Do Any of These Resonate with You?

If you're feeling stuck about articulating your values, consider the following list:

- acceptance
- adventure
- authenticity
- balance
- community
- compassion
- connection
- courage
- creativity
- credibility
- curiosity
- discipline
- diversity
- enthusiasm
- faith
- family
- forgiveness
- friendship
- health
- honesty
- humor
- insightfulness
- integrity
- justice
- learning
- loyalty
- mastery
- peace
- resilience
- respect
- service
- spiritualism
- wisdom

Need more inspiration? Visit the Box of Life Resources page at oritramler. com for additional values you may identify with more closely.

Boxing Our Values

Values are key to our essence, but they can also be quite abstract. How can we capture ideas like integrity or compassion or respect in our boxes? There are innumerable ways.

One of them is sharing stories. In order to capture his value of accountability, one of my coaching clients, Sebastian, is audio recording reflections of times he had to admit he was wrong. The first story describes when he was ten years old, broke his brother's bike, and didn't say a word about it. Unfortunately, his neighbor saw him and told his mom. His parents were more upset about him hiding what he did than actually breaking the bike. That's when he learned how important accountability is. He shared another story about when, as an adult, he made a mistake at work that almost caused a major profit loss. He immediately called for an emergency meeting that not only brought great minds together to help him solve the problem he caused, but it also resulted in a better outcome than the one originally forecasted.

When Joanne was putting her box together, she told me, "I'm including a branch of a plant I've had for over fifty years. It reminds me of the importance of the natural world in my life."

Tania ranks philanthropy high among her values. She is including in her box the mission statement of every organization she supports, along with the names of the people sitting on the boards. As she explains her logic, "I've seen too many organizations that distance themselves from their original mission based on the people on their boards. When someone looks into my box when I'm gone, I want to make sure they understand why I once gave to that organization and who was at the helm at the time."

- Identify the core values that you currently would like represented in your Box of Life. In other words, what kind of person are you, and what do you want others to know about the person you are?
- If you're boxing for someone else, what would you say their core values are? How did these manifest?
- Draft a timeline of your values throughout your life to include in your box.
- In what ways do you act on your values? Share three experiences in your life during which you lived your values.

Life Purpose and *Kavanah*

The Hebrew word *kavanah* encompasses intention, concentration, focus, and feeling. In the Jewish tradition, embracing *kavanah* has an impact on the way we live our lives through meaningful actions. Charles called this "focusing on living." In his box, I found more than one article where Charles was quoted saying, "To those who want to get to ninety and beyond, focus on living." As he put it, "Orit, I don't live on autopilot. I navigate my life by being at the helm of my circumstances and making the most out of it." Charles constantly engaged in activities that enhanced his day-to-day by providing him with personal enrichment and fulfillment.

Like Charles, I believe that each one of us is the engineer of our own life. As I was wrapping up the first draft of this book, I had a vivid dream in which all people had a designated supervisor whose job was to ensure we added something meaningful every day to our Box of Life. If the supervisor noticed that we didn't do it, we had to relive that day but with more intention, or *kavanah*. I woke up fascinated by the dream and kept analyzing it. On one hand, it would be overwhelming to add something every single day and would defeat the purpose of carefully curating what we include in our box. On the other hand, the thought of living every day in a way that creates memorable moments and enrichment is intriguing. Why the need for a supervisor? It is good to have someone who holds us accountable. I smiled at that realization because that's what I do as a coach: I hold my clients accountable.

Inspired by both Charles and my dream, I challenged myself—and now I challenge you—to *focus on living*. Every night before going to sleep, ask yourself, "What did I accomplish in the last 24 hours?" And then—acknowledging that there will always be things out of your control—make a commitment to living intentionally and determining what you want to accomplish the next day.

A friend sent me an anonymous quotation that reads, "The day that I understood that the only thing I will take away with me is what I have lived, I started to live what I want to take away with me." For me, that means living with *kavanah* in all dimensions of my life. Every New Year, I remind myself that one year equals 365 opportunities, and what we do every day matters more than what we do occasionally. Aristotle reminded us, "You are what you repeatedly do." The same applies to your Box of Life—what you include more of is what will reveal who you truly are and how you focus on living.

> *"The purpose of life is a life of purpose."*
> —Robert Byrne

Reflect and Take Action

- What is your purpose in life? To help you answer this question, consider your values, stories, mottos, and how you live your life every day.
- How will this purpose show up in your box? Consider creating a personal mission statement that will reflect your purpose.

Grit, Passion, and Purpose

Charles told me on several occasions, "There are no accidents in life." I too am a strong believer that things always happen for a reason. Given this faith and trust that everything presented to him had a purpose, Charles met challenges and new experiences with fierce passion and enthusiasm.

He could be the poster child for "grit" as defined by American psychologist Angela Lee Duckworth, author of *Grit: The Power of Passion and Perseverance*. The book outlines five characteristics—courage, conscientiousness, perseverance, resilience, and passion—that together make up grit, and Charles embodied all of them. Duckworth's research shows that passionate people have a deep sense of purpose. They also know themselves—they have a clear sense of their values and beliefs and they live by them. They generally accept themselves as imperfect and growing, contemplating a series of choices and options. They are driven by goals and are result-oriented. They don't let anything stop them and don't accept "no" for an answer. Passionate people recognize that they are in the driver's seat as they travel along their journey through life.

To understand how Charles exemplified grit, I'd like to share a story I found in his box (which also speaks to his creativity). As a child, Charles loved sculpting. He would spend countless hours carving dogs from bars of Ivory soap, perfecting his art. His dad, a very strict, traditional man, did not believe Charles would ever make a living as an artist, and he heavily discouraged Charles from seriously pursuing his artistic dreams. Charles obeyed his father's wishes, following a more traditional career path. But he kept the artist in him alive. For his sixty-fifth birthday, he took a trip to New Mexico with Mildred and reconnected with his love for sculpting. Charles explained, "Each person seeks immortality in their own unique way. I've been many things in my life and had various careers, but being a sculptor is the only lasting thing that will give me recognition in the future."

In an interview I found in his box, Charles describes how he came across a man who was carving a piece of stone with a knife: "I asked him what he was doing. When he said he was cutting stone, I said, 'But you're cutting stone with a knife! What kind of stone is it?' The man responded, 'Soapstone. It's soft enough to cut with a knife.' I was intrigued. I found out I could get the stone at Kaya Manga Stone Works in Santa Fe and bought a large piece of it. Next, we went to the supermarket and bought a paring knife. I figured, I was on vacation and . . . this could be an interesting beginning. And so, I carved my first piece of sculpture at sixty-five. An accident? I don't think so."

At first Charles focused on abstract stone sculptures that he cast in bronze. He wanted to create "monuments in miniature." At one point Mildred said, "The cutting of the stone is fine . . . but do you realize how many thousands of dollars you have already spent? Why don't you find out if somebody will want them, buy them, or use them? Why don't you pack them and put them in the car, and the next time we pass a gallery we go in and find out if they would like to see them?" Reluctantly, that's what Charles did, and his pieces landed in Art Incorporated, the largest art gallery in San Antonio. Before long, someone saw his sculpture there and arranged for a show at a gallery in Dallas, which opened many other doors.

Charles's interview continues: "One of my patrons was a physician, and he had purchased two or three pieces of my sculpture, and one day he said to me, 'My father is going to be celebrating his eightieth birthday and I would like to give him a Hebrew letter that really exemplifies his life.' I said, 'What letter are you talking about?' He said, 'The *gimel*,' and I said, 'Oh, the *gimel*.' I could read Hebrew, I could *daven* (the word for pray in Hebrew), but I really didn't know the meaning of the words . . . So I said, 'Well you know, I'm hesitant to take a commission because I don't know I can fulfill it, but I will try . . .' In the paper I saw that Rabbi Hayim Pinchas, a Torah scribe on the meaning of the Hebrew letters, was coming to visit a congregation in San Antonio, where they were writing letters in the Torah (Judaism sacred text) . . . I listened to him . . . and I went absolutely out of my mind."

After attending Rabbi Pinchas's lecture, Charles fell in love with the Hebrew alphabet. He began to see the letters as profound, primal, and spiritual forces, and he decided to learn more about them and to sculpt them. He claimed that the letters changed his life by providing him with a deeper spirituality. Charles's beautiful Hebrew letters were exhibited in many prominent locations. One of them can be seen at Yeshiva University in New York to this day.

The story of Charles and his late career in sculpting is a good reminder that we must not miss opportunities to discover and pursue our true interests. Curiosity, perseverance, and a good dose of *chutzpah* can transport us to good places.

> *"Every child is an artist. The problem is how to remain an artist once he grows up."*
> —Pablo Picasso

A photograph Charles gave me as a gift. It includes his sculpture of the eighteenth letter of the Hebrew alphabet, the letter *tzadik*, which stands for "righteousness, a man at his highest level, the connection between man and God," according to Charles's own description.

Personal Life Philosophy

My life philosophy can be summarized in one phrase: make it a good one. I've learned that life is good only if I make it so. No matter what life throws at us, we need to make the choice to be proactive and empowered to make it a good one for us and for others.

I discovered this as a child growing up in Israel. I remember missile alarms waking us up in the middle of the night during the Yom Kippur War in 1973. We rushed to the bomb shelters where we'd find yummy snacks, people playing guitars, board games, and lots of other things to help the little ones feel safe. The mindset everyone had was to make the best out of a tough and scary situation. This philosophy was cemented later when I moved from country to country. Each time, I had two choices: either *make it a good one* and integrate myself, or surrender myself to feeling isolated and stuck, longing for what I had left behind.

Choosing to make it a good one is acknowledging that life is not good or bad, but rather life brings what life brings: good, bad, and everything in between. It is on us to make the best of it. Yes, even when everything feels dark around us, even while grieving a loss, we can bring light into our lives by connecting with the meaning of our experience. It is not an easy task, but with proper effort and support, most of the time we can get there. In the words of American novelist Louisa May Alcott, "Painful as it may be, a significant emotional event can be a catalyst for choosing a direction that serves us—and those around us—more effectively. Look for the learning."

Charles once asked me what making a good life meant. I remember explaining that there are as many answers to that question as there are people on earth. For some, a good life is the adrenaline rush that comes from thrill and danger, while for others, it is total serenity and sense of security. For some, it is about their faith. For some, a good life revolves around family and connection, while for others it is found in solitude. Some say it is about making a lot of money and enjoying it, while others strive for simplicity. Some seek love and a family, while others want to explore the world with absolute freedom.

One thing is for sure: making your life a good one is not about creating a world of constant happiness. This does not exist. Instead, it is about fashioning a life of purpose and fulfillment within a world of imperfections. That is what Charles did when he talked to the person carving stone with a knife, or when he decided to go to a lecture about a personal interest and then pursue that interest. He was designing his life.

Reflect and Take Action

- What do you do to make your life a good one? Identify five things that you can include in your box to reflect this. For example, think about how you react when faced with a challenge in order to gain a new perspective, what you do to treat yourself or others to something special, or which stories or quotes inspire you.

Make It a Good One

The way I see it, someone who makes their life a good one is someone who

✓ has a sense of meaning and purpose—*Kavanah*,

✓ knows their values and acts accordingly,

✓ seeks and speaks the truth,

✓ stands up for what is just,

✓ finds value in practicing whatever they want to be good at,

✓ uses their inner strength to make healthy choices,

✓ is accountable for their actions and thoughts,

✓ feels a part of something greater than themselves,

✓ is open and respectful to people and ideas different from their own,

✓ knows the importance of a smile and the meaning of a hug,

✓ looks you in the eye.

Personal Motto

Make it a good one serves not only as a life philosophy but also as a motto for me, which I find useful. Having a motto keeps me directed toward my goals and core values. According to the Merriam-Webster dictionary, a motto is "a sentence, phrase, or word inscribed on something as appropriate to or indicative of its character or use; a short expression of a guiding principle." It serves as a guide to one's conduct by acting as a quick reminder of what's important, who we are, and what we stand for. As an example, one well-known motto belongs to Gandhi, who said, "Be the change you wish to see in the world."

Can you think of a motto to guide your life? What are a few words that can sum up your outlook and help keep you pointed toward your goals?

When choosing your motto, I have two recommendations:

1. Keep it short and easy to remember. It can be one word, such as "kind," or a phrase, such as "No pain, no gain," "Always learning," or "Practice gratitude."
2. Make it so it strikes the right chord within you. It must remind you of what's important to you, who you are, and what you stand for.

Sense of Purpose

Our values, outlook, and personal philosophy can help us determine our purpose, or the central, motivating aim in our life. This is a moving target— our sense of purpose and fulfillment is always evolving. By welcoming challenges as they appear, grieving our losses when they occur, embracing opportunities when they arise, and taking actions that define our purpose in life—our *kavanah*—we can reach fulfillment.

In Charles's box I found a piece of paper that read: "In the 1940s, Viktor Emil Frankl, an Austrian neurologist, psychiatrist, philosopher, and author, was held prisoner in Nazi concentration camps. With all the agony and brutality, what kept Frankl from giving up was purpose! Frankl found meaning in his struggle, and that's what gave him the power to push forward through unimaginable pain. That's what gave him the power to survive hell, without losing the will to live."

When coaching my clients and asking them where their sense of purpose and fulfillment comes from, I've found an interesting variety of answers:

- knowing I have a calling that is bigger than myself
- living by my values and beliefs
- following my passions
- embracing my family
- learning new things
- making a difference
- being at the helm of my life
- observing the wonders of nature
- practicing my faith
- knowing that the only way is forward
- playing soccer with my team

You might be wondering how you know what your purpose is, or what brings you true fulfillment. Figuring it out can certainly feel daunting. A good place to start is by asking yourself, What makes your heart tick? What do you care about the most? Your core values can help answer this question as well. Think about what motivates you to get up in the morning (besides the alarm clock). If your answer is, "Going to work makes me wake up every morning," dig deeper and ask yourself, "Why do I go to work?" Keep asking why until you get to an answer that is greater than yourself and those around you.

Another way to approach this is to ask yourself, "If I found out that I only had a year to live, how would I live my life?" It is not pleasant to think about our death; it is frightening. But it forces us to zero in on what matters most to us. We are pushed to reevaluate our priorities. Those priorities dictate not only how we live but also what stories we will be remembered by.

A term that can help us think about our life purpose is *ikigai* (Japanese for "a reason for being"). *Iki* in Japanese means life, and *gai* describes value or worth. It is a concept referring to something that gives a person a sense of purpose, fulfillment, and a reason for living. *Ikigai* is the common ground between what we love, what we are good at, and what enables us to express our morals and values. In 2005, *New York Times* bestselling author Dan Buettner wrote a cover story for *National Geographic* on the secret of longevity centered around "Blue Zones." A Blue Zone is a region where people are healthier and live longer than anywhere else on the planet. His research led him to believe that *ikigai* may be one of the reasons for the longevity of the people of Okinawa, a Japanese island in the East China Sea. Okinawans have less desire to retire and continue to work as long as they remain healthy. Buettner explains, "If you don't know where you are going in life, then you're never going to get there. *Ikigai*—and being able to articulate your *ikigai*—gives you a destination." To find your *ikigai*, Dan recommends that you sit down with a piece of paper, or at a computer screen, and make three columns.[1] At the top of the first column, write "What I love to do." The second column should say "What I'm good at," and the third column should say "What allows me to live my values." Make a long list for each of those. Your *ikigai* is the cross section between all three, and you want to make sure you have an outlet for that in your life.

> *"And in the end, it is not the years in your life; that count. It is the life in your years."*
> —Abraham Lincoln

Reflect and Take Action

- What three examples can you share of times you did something that shaped your life?

---

[1] Stuart Kenny. "Ikigai: The Secret to a Longer and Happier Life," *Red Bull*, 22 Jan. 2019, https://www.redbull.com/za-en/ikigai-japanese-concept-secrets.

- Create a timeline of how your sense of purpose and fulfillment has evolved over the years.
- Think of five things that you can include in your box that will reflect your life purpose and philosophy.
- If someone had to guess your life purpose just from looking at your Box of Life, what would they guess?
- If you're boxing for someone else, think about what you'd say their purpose was. If you can, ask them what they'd say it is.

We all have a purpose in life, but many times we just aren't aware of what it is. Our boxes can help reveal that purpose by looking at what we are preserving as our story. Charles's purpose was revealed in his box: it was about constantly re-creating himself to further his personal and professional development. My purpose is to create deep connections and memorable moments. It is represented in my box with snapshots of the people I'm connecting with and descriptions of those moments.

> *"Meaning is not something you stumble across, like the answer to a riddle or the prize to a treasure hunt. Meaning is something you build into your life. You build it out of your past, out of your affections and loyalties, out of the experience of humankind as it is passed on to you, out of your own talent and understanding, out of the things you believe in, out of the things and people you love, out of the values for which you are willing to sacrifice something."*
> —John W. Gardner

Chapter 6

How We Spend Our Time

"In truth, people can generally make time for what they choose to do; it is not the time but the will that is wanting."

—John Lubbock

In his check-in calls, Charles used to ask me, "So, Orit, how are you planning to invest your time today?" With that question alone he could help me refocus and regain purpose to my day.

There is a big difference between passing our time and *investing* our time. When we *pass* our time, we are using the time we have for the sake of letting it slip away, not expecting anything in return besides the passage of time itself. Sometimes this has its value, like when you just need to take a breath. However, it's a red flag if that's the most prevalent way we live our lives. On the other hand, when we *invest* our time, we engage in something that we believe will bring us a meaningful reward.

When I asked Charles why he chose the word "invest" when asking about my time, he said, "Orit, imagine life as a bank. Our bank account is our life, and time is our currency." Since then, I like to visualize my account balance by reviewing my investing and spending. The more I spend, the more I deplete my account in exchange for instant gratification. The more I invest, the more the future value of my account increases, often in exchange for delayed, yet ultimately more meaningful, gratification. This thought experiment can help me understand my biggest expenses (in units of time), identify which areas of life I invest in, and paint a picture of my future. If I don't like what I see, adjustments can be made accordingly. I mainly invest my active time in family, work, friends, community, and personal and professional development. On those days when the only thing I do is work, I know my account needs to be rebalanced. It all comes back to living with *kavanah*.

When we invest our time well, in return we will

- feel a sense of accomplishment and pride,
- develop our personal and professional growth,
- find solutions to our struggles and move forward,
- benefit from having more meaningful and healthier relationships,
- let go of what's not important,
- implement self-care and improve well-being,
- have more moments of enjoyable leisure without guilt,
- do more of the things we enjoy, and,
- feel fulfilled.

"We think much more about the use of money, which is renewable, than we do about the use of time, which is irreplaceable."
—Jean-Louis Servan-Schreiber

The Art of Doing Nothing

I asked Bella, a client leading a successful start-up while also starting a family, how she manages to always look so put-together and calm. She said she invests some of her busy schedule every week "doing nothing." She explained, "I'm from an Italian background, and Italians have mastered this idea. Back in Italy, my dad would close his shop after lunch for his *riposo*. *Riposo* is the afternoon shutdown for an hour or so every day after lunch. He was then reenergized to keep going. I don't have that luxury every day, but I make sure I do it at least once a week. That's a sacred time in which I don't look at my cell phone or computer, I don't work, and I don't run errands. I just do whatever will reenergize me to keep going, and I do it without guilt because I planned for it."

Bella shared that she is including a sample of her weekly planner in her box. Her *riposo* is clearly marked on her calendar, and she hopes that one day when her daughters—who will hopefully also be successful professionals—wonder how she did it all, they will realize that spending time doing nothing can ultimately make you more efficient and help you accomplish your goals.

Our Work

At a high level, humans around the globe spend their time on similar activities—work, rest, and leisure. And for many of us, work takes up a good chunk of our non-resting hours. I'm referring to work as any activity involving mental or physical effort done to achieve a purpose or result. It can be paid or unpaid and may include raising kids, running a household, volunteering, and regularly helping a neighbor. It can be anything that occupies our time beyond rest or fun. One study showed that over the course of a lifetime, the average worker spends nearly a quarter of their time on the job during a typical fifty-year stint of employment. At times we may feel that we spend more hours at work than at home (at least before COVID, which introduced remote working as a viable option for many). We spend so much time working that, for many of us, it becomes an essential part of how we define ourselves. It affects our general mood and our life outcomes. So it's no surprise that our occupation plays a central role in our Box of Life.

Charles's box was no exception: his work had the biggest presence. Work was a key aspect of how Charles defined himself. Whether it was as a businessman, publisher, artist, activist, or volunteer, his box was populated with materials that spoke to those roles. Charles always expressed pride about his work. Through his box he made sure that I became aware of each initiative he engaged with through photos, articles he wrote, letterheads he created, and his many professional business cards.

Robert, a physical therapist, is including letters of appreciation that former clients wrote to him in his box. "I keep them because they remind me that the work I do matters," he said. Tina, a school administrator, is putting mementos of achievements and fun times in her box. "I have photos of me and my work friends, annual reviews I want to remember, invitations to events I helped put on, a printout of weeks of my work calendar—stuff like that. My hope is that it shows a full picture of my work life, which is a big part of who I am." Craig, a veterinarian, is keeping a notebook in which he writes every Friday about his work. "The life of a veterinarian is filled with drama, humor, and love—perhaps much like any other human profession, but more. There is no boring week for me. Perhaps one day the notebook in my box will become a book," Craig explained.

In my box, I'm commemorating my work and volunteerism by including appreciation messages I received from emerging leaders, board members, and other people who I worked with or volunteered with over the years. I'm also including my résumé, photos, articles about my work, and copies of my LinkedIn testimonials.

What we choose as our career speaks to our values, as does how we distribute our time among different daily demands. Don't we generally ask people we meet, "What do you do?" instead of "Who are you?" Take a moment to reflect on how your work defines you and your life.

A Career Box of Life

I recently had the opportunity to work with a client named Sebastian. At age fifty-one, he had been working in his field for fifteen years and was thinking about making a change. Per my request, he collected the most important moments in his career, and together we created a Box of Life to reflect his professional accomplishments, turning points, adversities, and successes. Once we were done, he gained a better perspective on his career and an understanding of what made him unique professionally. With a sense of relief, he shared, "Wow! I just realized that there are many things I've done and forgotten about, although they were pivotal building blocks in my career. I like what I can now see, thanks to this box, and have a better understanding of what I have to offer."

This meeting with Sebastian reminded me how the exercise of creating a box reconnects us with our unique attributes and abilities and provides us with the tools we need to stand out in whatever endeavor we decide to pursue. The same is true for organizations and teams who put their boxes together to preserve institutional memory—in the process they come to also understand their value and accomplishments.

- How do you invest your time? Look at your calendar and identify the time you invest in work, yourself, and in others, as well as the activities you do on a regular basis. How does your list make you feel? Is there anything you can adjust or need to do less or more of?

- Consider making a work timeline. You can use a résumé as a substitute, but a timeline could include jobs that don't fit on your professional résumé (including the gigs you had as a kid, like babysitting, mowing lawns, or scooping ice cream). It can also be a lot more personal, including photos, what you liked and disliked about the job, funny memories, and more.

- List your five proudest achievements related to your occupation.

- List your hobbies or special interests. Create a timeline with photos of how those hobbies evolved over time.

- If someone were to open your Box of Life today, what would they conclude about how you are investing your time? Why?

The Path Not Taken

While having dinner with friends once, my husband started a fascinating conversation by asking people around the table what they would like to be if there were a "redo." I was surprised when my friend Elizabeth said, "A florist." She began to describe the shop she visualized and the flower arrangements she would create, and as she was doing so, her face became more and more radiant. No one around that table answered the question by simply saying, "The same thing I am doing now."

In my case, I love what I do, and yet I regret that I didn't follow my dream of becoming a psychiatrist. And in my next life? I would have a consulting business creating memorable moments for businesses and people. I would also be an interior designer on the side.

There are many different reasons, good and not so good, why most people don't end up following their passions. What's most important is how we can find ways to still do what we love, even if it is not through our main career. We can volunteer at organizations that are aligned with our true passions. We can take classes to develop skills we want to have. The path not taken once can still be taken at a different highway exit, just as Charles did. He self-taught himself music at an old age and became the artist he always wanted to be.

The Hats We Wear

Charles reinvented himself many times throughout his lifetime. Inside his box I found evidence of the many hats he wore—the roles that he chose and the roles that life handed to him. In his own words, "I don't believe in excuses, and I never saw a limitation on my ability to accomplish what I wanted to accomplish, no matter my knowledge of the matter or even my age." In the cases that Charles did fail in a role, which happened to him more than once, he would be disappointed for a while but then say, "At least I tried it," and move on to the next thing. And of course, not all of his hats had to do with work. We all fill many roles that involve a variety of tasks.

The following are some of the hats Charles wore over the course of his life:

- chemical sales manager and consultant
- radio talk show host
- activist
- philanthropist
- sculptor
- caregiver
- actor
- scriptwriter

Charles acting

- TV personality
- oil painter
- board member
- volunteer
- PR professional
- marketing-sales professional
- motivational speaker
- entrepreneur
- mentor to journalists, authors, seniors, and businesswomen
- son
- father
- husband
- friend
- congregant
- community member
- cartoonist

As you can see, that's quite a diverse list! In an interview I found in his box, Charles said, "What most people perceive as social, emotional, physical, or economic boundaries are usually no more than mental boundaries they impose on themselves. I never bought into these boundaries because I knew it would only be detrimental to my own fulfillment and eventual success." Any idea, opportunity, or project that made Charles's heart tick, he would simply jump into.

But it wasn't only his jobs that defined the richness and fulfillment of his life, it was all the other things he did that gave him a strong sense of self-worth. And when he could occasionally make a living through his passions, that was only a bonus.

The archive of my adult life doesn't feel as wide ranging as Charles's, but when I sat down to list my own hats, past and current, I was surprised by how many there were:

- mother
- daughter
- wife
- family member
- dog guardian
- friend
- learning specialist
- special needs professional
- entrepreneur
- business owner
- certified coach
- consultant
- executive director
- fundraiser
- board member
- congregant
- community member
- activist
- philanthropist
- volunteer
- volunteer coordinator
- youth counselor
- connector
- youth-movement director
- camp director
- neighbor
- trainer and facilitator
- event organizer
- sports fan
- caregiver

And now I can add . . .

- author

Making this list surprised me in a positive way. I came to the realization that I'm investing my time relatively well, especially when I think about what each hat has given me. The exercise also made me think of the hats I wish were in my box—and now that I'm aware, I'm going for them! I want to explore adding the following hats: artist, golfer (I'll give it a try at least), TED Talk speaker, cook, world traveler, amateur interior designer, creator of memorable moments, influencer, and grandmother (no pressure, kids!).

Reflect and Take Action

- Create a list of all the hats you are wearing or have worn in the past. Consider adding pictures for every hat.

- Now list all the hats that you hope to wear in the future. If you can, add pictures—visualizing goals helps to make them happen!
- If you're boxing for someone else, help them determine all the hats they've worn in the past and continue to wear today.

Continuous Learning

Journalist and entrepreneur Michael Simmons researched what behaviors are shared by the most successful people in the world, and he found that no matter how busy they are, ultra-successful people devote at least five hours per week to deliberate learning. As a result of this finding, he coined the "five-hour rule"[1] and traced it all the way back to Benjamin Franklin, a notorious learner. Franklin consistently woke up early to read or write. He created lists of his goals so he could monitor his progress. He embraced experiments to test ideas. He asked difficult questions or discussed things he found interesting. Today, successful people follow the same principles of reading, writing, reflecting, meditating, and experimenting.

I'm the first to acknowledge that many of us lead busy lives with hectic schedules. Usually, we start our day bright and early, and at the end of what often feels like an exhausting workday, we still need to run errands, do laundry, cook, eat, take care of those who depend on us, and spend quality time with loved ones. The idea of adding one more thing to our plate can be overwhelming. But learning takes many forms—it can be reading, listening to an audiobook, podcasts, or TED Talks, interviewing people, or taking a class. And what we learn can energize and enrich us, making the time we invest well worthwhile.

---

[1] Simmons, Michael. "Why Constant Learners All Embrace the 5-Hour Rule." *Michael Simmons*, michaelsimmons.com/why-constant-learners-all-embrace-the-5-hour-rule-mm09.

Does Time Fly?

As a coach, I speak to a variety of people:

- **Timeless:** These people can't find enough hours in a day to do what they need to do and feel overwhelmed. They complain that "time flies because there is not enough of it."

- **Timeful:** These people don't know what to do with their time or are busy but bored. They complain that "time is eternal."

- **Timewise:** These are people like Charles. They are always busy doing what they need to do and what they want to do, and they are almost never bored or overwhelmed.

Can you identify with any of the people categories above? Every single one of us has exactly the same "time budget": 24 hours per day, 365 days per year, which amounts to 8,760 hours *every year of our lives*. That's how much time we have to do what we need and want to do. The question is, Are we making the most of the 1,440 minutes that we all have available every day?

There is no doubt that the lucky ones are those who are like Charles, folks whose outlook keeps them engaged with the world. For the most part, it's not about how much they have on their plate, it's about their attitude toward it. Instead of becoming overwhelmed or harried by the challenges they face, they take them in stride. Instead of becoming bored by the tedious aspects of life, they accept them and move on. At the end of the day, it is all about your outlook on life that makes time fly or crawl.

- Think about times when you were involved in situations or activities that made time fly because you were engaged and loving what you were doing. What was going on? Was there anyone else with you? How can you do more of that? Those situations and activities deserve a place in your box.

Retirement Is a Relative Term

When Charles reached his eightieth birthday, he wrote, "Life begins at eighty," which became one of his favorite statements. At that age, Charles still added to his box and built his legacy. He called himself a "seasoned citizen" instead of a "senior citizen." He still invested his time the way he always had, creating new stories to tell, starting new projects, and appreciating life until his final days and beyond.

I personally believe that life begins the day we are born, and then it begins again every day when we are given the blessing of waking up. It also begins at every new stage in life. As Charles wrote in an article, "Older people are sometimes their own worst enemies because of their attitudes. They think they've reached a certain place in the proverbial pecking order of the workplace and that they are stuck there. But that's just not true. What you were yesterday you may not be today. You may be different—and better."

Once retirement came, Charles continued to live a very active life. "Retirement is a relative term," he would say. It appears Charles tried to retire at least five times, and each time he discovered a new interest, which he eventually commercialized and turned into a new "career."

Pat, a former client and a successful artist who works with ceramics, once told me, "I need help retiring. I always say I will, but for some mysterious reason I don't." My response was, "Have you considered the fact that maybe you can't retire because you can't retire from who you are?" That was an *aha* moment for Pat. She was one of those lucky people who can make a living just out of who they truly are. Pat just had to keep doing what she loved but perhaps adjust her goals and expectations from considering it a "job" to considering it simply something she loved doing. Pat continued making ceramics, but she worked at a gentler pace and just for the fun of it while enjoying time with her grandchildren and friends. In her box, Pat has a ceramic tile with one of my sayings—an "Oritism," as she put it—that reads, "Do who you are."

Reflect and Take Action

- What can't you retire from?
- What would you like to be doing at eighty years old? What do you need to do today so you can get there?

How We Spend Our Time Is Who We Are

In any box, the story of how we invested our time in the past and how we invest it today is one that I treasure, as it speaks directly to our values. In my box, you will learn about my time with family first and foremost. You will also learn about my time with friends and my community engagement. You will learn about my jobs, which have luckily always been aligned with who I am and have empowered me to flow every single day, even those days when the work was challenging. You will encounter my hobbies, which I don't do enough of yet. You will discover the things I've learned and will keep learning that keep me curious and current. You will meet all my beloved pets in whom I also invest my time, and you might even find a few tickets to Carolina Hurricanes hockey games and to Duke basketball games, and *if* I am lucky enough one day, to an Argentinean World Cup soccer game (which is still on my bucket list).

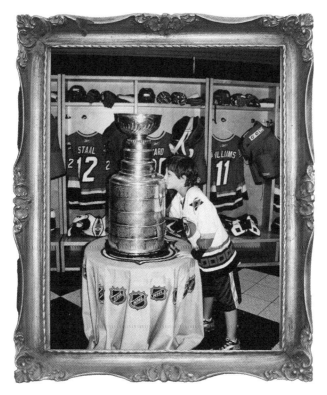

A photo of my son kissing the Stanley Cup in 2006 when our team, the Carolina Hurricanes, won it all!

> *"You are never too old to set another goal or to dream a new dream."*
> —C.S. Lewis

Chapter 7

Family

"Families are like branches on a tree. We grow in different directions,
yet our roots remain as one."

—Anonymous

My family is the most important thing in my life. The well-being of my husband, kids, mother, and dogs internally guides me in every decision, action, and breath I take. Put simply, their well-being is *my* well-being. And I'm far from alone in this. A 2021 Pew Research Center survey found that Americans listed family the number one thing that makes life meaningful.[1]

Families are the building blocks of many individuals' lives, and family values are reflected in society at large. Families serve as microcosms for larger social issues. Our collective Boxes of Life could become an interesting sociological tool for research when exploring what we each included about our families and our family values. Sociologists might be interested in understanding how you think about your family and its role in your life.

---

[1]   Laura Silver, et al. "What Makes Life Meaningful? Views from 17 Advanced Economies." Https://Www.Pewreaserch.Org/Global/2021/11/18/What-Makes-Life-Meaningful-Views-from-17-Advanced-Economies/, November 18, 2021.

Our boxes might reflect different family structures; how our family interacts with other institutions such as schools, businesses, and government agencies; and how all these factors affect children growing up in the family. After all, family is one of the most important parts of our lives. It's where we learn how to be a good citizen, and it's the main source of our value formulation.

I try to create as many memorable moments with my family as feasibly possible, whether through meals, conversations, vacations, or celebrations. However, family is about much more than just enjoying moments and quality time together. Family forms who we are. Who we are today is often the result of who our family members were in the past. As Zen Master Tich Nhat Hanah once said, "If you look deep into the palm of your hand, you will see your parents and all generations of your ancestors. All of them are alive in this moment. Each is present in your body. You are the continuation of each of those people." In our family roots and history, we find explanations for our personality traits, values, and behaviors. I believe that our personal stories and our family stories are woven together, shaping each other. Where we are going is important, but knowing where we came from is just as important.

Thus, for many of us, families will play a significant role in our boxes—we'll share our relationships and history, whether it's birthdays or holidays or just a simple Sunday dinner at Grandma's house.

A Broader Definition of Family

"Family isn't always blood. It's the people in your life who want you in theirs. The ones who accept you for who you are. The ones who would do anything to see you smile and who love you no matter what."

—often credited to Maya Angelou

As the quotation above attests, our family is not only the one we were born into or defined by our genes, birth certificate, and last name. Our family is also the one we build, the one that chooses us, and the one we choose. A strong bond, such as in certain friendships, in which loyalty, care, and affection prevail, can also define a family.

Reflect and Take Action

- In one quick sentence, describe what family means to you.
- What three things have you learned about being part of a family?
- What are some stories and myths that run in your family? How would you include them in your box?

Family First

I don't think it's right, or even possible, to turn your back on family. For better or worse, we are carrying them with us just by being who we are. I believe family brings with it a commitment to care about members, regardless of whether you like or dislike them as individuals. Some family members you're compatible with, others can be difficult, or worse. Some shower you with appreciation and love, while others show little to no affection or take you for granted. But simply by virtue of being family, we must show them consideration.

Judaism teaches us that when it comes to charity, our first responsibility is toward family. "A poor person who is his relative comes before all others," writes the Rambam, a medieval Jewish philosopher. While we are obligated to help the poor, there is a special responsibility to support and maintain one's own family.

Of course, life and humans are complicated, and there are always exceptions to the rules. Sometimes it's healthier to let go of certain family relationships, but I genuinely believe that if everyone in the world shared the understanding that family comes first, the world would be a better place— one with less anxiety, violence, bullying, and even terrorism. I believe such a micro-level commitment and dedication to the people we call our family could have a macro-level influence on the greater society.

Reflect and Take Action

- Have you made sacrifices for your family? In what ways have you set aside other goals to put family first?
- Do you have, or have you had, a complicated relationship with a relative that you would like to share when creating your box?

Our Parents

No matter what your relationship with your parents looks like, it's almost certain that they are among the most influential people in your life. Our parents are our first teachers and we learn an immense amount from them, often without being aware of it. If you're fortunate, your parents are also a source of guidance, support, and love.

Charles's face always lit up when speaking about his father and mother, and he shared many memories with me about how his dad's mandates influenced him, even when they contradicted what he himself wanted. His mother seemed to be more supportive of his endeavors.

Ina, Charles's daughter, referenced how much she'd learned from her parents in a speech she gave for their fiftieth anniversary: "What a pair they are! The inveterate, ebullient salesman and the steadfast, strong-willed teacher. How much they've learned from each other over the years and how much they've taught me—especially about the importance of family and friends . . . We Sterns are a small family, but our diverse personalities loom large, and we've challenged each other in many ways over the years. Thank God we've all made an effort to appreciate our differences—it's made us close and it's kept us friends."

My own parents have always been there for me. Throughout my life, I relied on them for guidance and support. They taught me right from wrong and helped me navigate the world. They were the ones who comforted me when I cried, cheered for me when I succeeded, and held me when I was feeling down.

My dad set high expectations for me—he pushed me to always be the best version of myself. My mom was always there to make sure that I felt like I could do anything and that I was the most accomplished person in the world. They complemented each other well. Their love was always unconditional. Their presence in my box and life is big. They weren't perfect parents—no one is! But knowing that they were the best version of parents they could have been, and as loving as parents can get . . . that's everything I need to know about them now.

I asked a diverse group of people who were putting their boxes together what the number one thing they learned from their parents was that they would like to preserve. In all cases, they complained that I only asked for one! Below are some of their answers:

- Don't make anyone feel invisible.
- Education is the door to hard work, and hard work is the door to success.

- Stand up for what's just.
- Live within your income and always save for stormy days.
- Be accountable for whatever you do.
- Never make assumptions.
- Take calculated risks to expand your comfort zone.
- Always give—only then will you get.
- Don't turn your back on your kids, even if you get divorced on terrible terms.
- Never get stuck or hide behind excuses.
- Don't lie to your family.

Lori, the CEO of a community foundation, told me, "My dad is my number one mentor. I've learned about work ethic, empathy, commitment, and about standing one's ground (although the last one is something I still need to work on). One of the biggest lessons he taught me was how to live and learn from disappointment. Throughout my childhood, he would say to me, 'If I could take away your pain or disappointment, I'd use every fiber of my being to do so, but I can't. I'm here to help you, but you need to figure out how to deal with it and come out on the other side.' He also likes to say, 'You can do anything for a little while.' I've reminded myself of this phrase often when dealing with a job or project or relationship that I was struggling with or didn't enjoy anymore."

When we think of our folks, it's easy to remember their roles as parents. We remember them making meals, teaching us how to ride a bike or drive a car, taking care of us when we were sick, and telling us to do better in school. But what about their roles as people? What did they bring to the table as individuals? Our boxes are about the things that made us who we are, and we all have things that came from our parents: traits like kindness or intelligence and personality quirks like stubbornness or persistence. Think about your personality traits and the lessons your parents imparted to you. Are they similar to the ones you'd like to impart to the next generation? Which of these lessons would you like to commemorate in your box?

- What don't you know about your parents that would make a difference to you? Is there anyone who could help you dig into that information?
- What are your family's top three values? How do these manifest?
- What five lessons have you learned from your parents? What difference have they made in your life?

When Your Parents Begin to Age

Honor your father and mother is a commandment that I've strived to follow throughout my life. At times it's difficult. Think about all the times your parents said "no" to something that was important to you, or when they weren't present when you needed them most, or when they disagreed with your life choices as you grew up and became an independent thinker.

That commandment can also be tough to follow when your parents age and become less self-sufficient, requiring more from you. It can be a struggle to shift from seeing them as pillars of support to becoming vulnerable and needing your support. These painful realities may be difficult to accept. Perhaps that's the reason there is a commandment to honor your parents—it's neither an obvious nor an easy task. We do it because it has to be done and because we remember when our parents were there for us unconditionally.

More important than supporting or doing favors for our parents is bringing quality to our relationships with them and creating as many memorable moments as we can. Investing our time with them is something we need to do because we can't take that time for granted. I always remember the words Charles told me from an anonymous source: "Love and appreciate your parents. We are often so busy growing up, we forget they are also growing old."

I received a letter from my mom the day I turned fifty. It is in my box and serves as a reminder to be patient every time I get a little frustrated with her slowing down and aging. Here is an abridgment:

My dearest Orit,

Feeling love is one of the most wonderful gifts that life gives us. Every time I look at you, a combination of my instinct, soul, mind, and heart makes me want to protect you and give you all the best that I can give you.

When you came into my life, everything changed. Having you near has been the greatest reward that life has given me. I'm grateful for being able to say I'm your mamá, something that has touched my core being and filled me with all good things . . .

I love you so much that even just the thought of how much I love you makes me emotional. I just hope I've raised you well . . . You know how to . . . make the most of everything that happens to you. You're creative and always strive to accomplish all your goals.

. . . I ask you that as years go by, be patient with me. I'll get a bit more tired, I'll forget some things, but I'll always keep being your mamá, feeling the same way as when they put you in my arms, and I'll always be by your side!

I love you infinitely!

Ima
01/31/2017

I must admit that patience has never been my strength, and it's hard for me to see my mom aging. Of course, my mom knows that—no wonder she made her request to me very clear, and while I know that aging is just a part of life, it still makes me sad. It reminds me that the end is coming in the same way that fall reminds me of a cold winter ahead. My mom's letter brought warmth to that winter, and every time I look into my box, that warmth will envelop me with her words of wisdom.

Reflect and Take Action

- What are three meaningful stories you remember about your childhood that involve one or both of your parents? Write these down.
- What do you want to remember most about your parents?
- What are three things that you believe you have accomplished because of your parents?
- Choose five things to put in your box that reflect your relationship with your parents at different stages of your life.

> *"When a newborn grips his father's finger with his little fist for the first time, he's got hold of him forever."*
> —Gabriel García Márquez

Creating a Box of Life for an Elderly Person

Creating a Box of Life for an elderly person is about collecting mementos and stories that hold meaning for them—or for you!—and that you want to keep close by. This could include sentimental items that represent who they are as a person, items that show how they lived their life and what they were passionate about, an album with pictures over the years, and personal items like jewelry, books, journals, and letters.

Here are some questions to consider when creating someone else's Box of Life:

- What are some of their favorite things (for example, places, activities, books, movies . . .)? Do they have any specialties or hobbies? What kind of music do they like? What kind of food do they love?
- What kind of work did they do? What were some of the highlights of their career?
- Who were the special people in their lives?
- What were some of their most memorable moments? What made those times so unique and memorable?

And remember to always attach a few lines to a photo or object, ideally sharing an anecdote and making it clear why you are including it in their box.

Our Children

My children are my universe. My world circles theirs, as the earth circles the sun. Am I overly focused on them? Maybe so. Whether it was Jane Fonda, Joe Paterno, or Sarah Payne Stuart who said, "You're only as happy as your least happy child," they knew what they were talking about.

Even if you don't have kids of your own, perhaps there are children in your life—nieces, nephews, or godchildren—who you know well and matter deeply to you. Children can enrich our lives in so many ways with their fresh perspectives, lack of self-consciousness, and the pleasure they take in simple things.

Charles's eyes shined every time he mentioned Ina, his daughter. His pride for her and her successful career was evident on his face. His worries about her personal fulfillment because of how much she worked came up in our conversations. As my son often reminds me, "Worrying is part of your job description as a parent." He is not wrong—being a parent means that you always need to be on your toes. But for me, it is also the most difficult yet beautiful and fulfilling "job" I have ever had.

In my Box of Life I've included a note I wrote for my children during their teenage years. I decided to include it in my box with the hope it will help them as parents as well. It reads:

```
What do I need as your mother?
    I need to know the truth. It is okay for me to
dislike it and to question it, but I need to know
always the truth. I need to trust you!
    I need to know that you can do what you said you
will do. Keep your promises and be accountable.
    I need to know that you won't follow those who
are making wrong choices just because you think
"everyone does it," or "it is cool," or just
because they are inviting you to join them. I
need to believe that you can stand proud of your
values and still have fun.
    I need to know that you are trying your best,
even when it is hard work and it takes away time
that can be spent in a more enjoyable way. I need
to know that you know that in life everything
requires effort and practice. If you do it now,
```

you will enjoy it later.

I need to know that when you are sad, or you feel that nothing is worth it anymore, you will remember that there is always another day to make things better. I need to know that you will find strength in the love of your family to overcome everything in life. I need to know that you know that I love you more than life itself.

I need your love here and there, a hug, a note, a sweet compliment.

I need your patience and understanding of me being different, older, your mom, worried, caring . . .

I need you to try hard to be nice to me as much as you can. I'm not a stranger and you can just be who you are around me, but I'm human and I have my own needs.

I need you to be that person you are that I love and admire.

Mami

Raising children consumes a significant chunk of our lives—it actually never ends! Throughout the years, we collect many memorable moments and anecdotes. Considering our emotional investment and the number of shared moments, choosing which ones we want to include in our box is not an easy task. While putting her children's boxes together, my young professional client, Debby, decided to create files titled My Firsts, Moments of Pride, Lessons Learned Together, Struggles, Memorable Moments, and Laughing Together. Another friend, Janet, has a Google Doc for each of her kids where she jots down favorite memories and family stories as they come up, pasting in photos when they exist.

A Parent's Love Is Forever

While working with Nathalie (ninety-four) on creating her box, she showed me a picture of her son who died in 1992 and wrote, "Michael, my middle child, was gay. I was aware of this from the time he was a little boy. For some reason, he did not know that I knew he was gay and was so afraid I would reject him. Gay shmay. He was my son and I LOVED him dearly. This was the 80s and AIDS was running rampant. He contracted the disease and had an excruciating period of illness. He fought it with all he had, but there was no cure . . . The last six weeks of his life I spent in New York. We finally got him back to his apartment on Friday, and he died the following Monday morning, never knowing he was out of the hospital. I had promised him that he would not die in the hospital."

She continued, "I'm not only including him in my box because I love him but also because I don't want anyone in our family to forget about him, as he won't have direct descendants like my other two children have. I want him to continue to be part of our family for generations to come. I also share that story because it is important that parents have that conversation that I didn't have, because I was assuming that he knew that I knew he was gay, but I was never clear enough about it. I wish I had been . . ." It broke my heart that every time Nathalie spoke about

The photo of Michael (may his memory be a blessing) that Nathalie included in her box

Michael, her tears burst like a fiercely erupting volcano. But then she told me, still with tears in her eyes, "Thank you for doing this with me. I haven't shared this much about Michael for a long time. I can feel him closer to me while doing this, and I feel I'm doing something important for him."

- What do you want the kids in your life to remember most about you?
- What are three things that you believe your kids, or other significant children in your life, have accomplished because of you?
- If you have children, choose five things to put in your box that reflect your relationship with them at different stages of their lives.
- Write a letter or record a short video of yourself speaking to each of the significant children in your life to include in your and their Boxes of Life.

Our Siblings

I'm an only child. If a fairy granted me a wish, without hesitation it would be to have a sibling. Yes, I acknowledge that many have shared that they don't have a good relationship with their siblings, but in my case, I want to believe I would have a great one. When I see siblings interact, I need to admit that in a healthy way, I feel extremely jealous.

It has not been easy to grow up without a sibling! I'm lucky I have my siblings by choice—my wonderful friends' and my husband's siblings—but at the end of the day they aren't able to share with me the "burdens" of being an only child. Believe me, we are not necessarily the "spoiled" ones we're made out to be. To the contrary, when all our parents' attention is just on us, the demands and expectations are higher than if we had to share our parents with others.

My sister-in-law Dalia opened her heart up when speaking about siblings. She wrote, "Throughout my life, my relationships with my siblings have been the most important . . . They are the refuge to which I always return to feel safe and loved. They are my support and most genuine source of love . . . I feel that we have a bond that overcomes distances, different points of view, and life philosophies.

I'm the third of five siblings, so I always felt as if I were in between two generations in our family: the youngest of the first and the oldest of the second. I think I hold a cross-generational place—one that allowed me to enjoy being cared for by my older siblings and one that "obligated" me to take care of and be responsible for my younger siblings. In this way, a safety net has been woven as a strong and permanent support in my life.

I associate adventures with my relationship to my brother—as the only male among four sisters, he's my adventure buddy. He taught me how to be bold but also to have fun . . .

With my sisters I treasure different moments, many that evoke feelings of complicity, as they are the keepers of my secrets. I trust them with my daughters' care, and we have endless chats on the phone: *Keep calm and call your sister* could be one of my mottos.

My siblings show up in my Box of Life as important protagonists through shared experiences and moments, but also as something much stronger that makes me myself. They are part of my universe, but also embody me."

Although I don't have the depth of connection like Dalia described, my husband's parents and sisters welcomed me as if I were one of them. I'll never forget the day I heard my oldest nephew, Julian, call me "tía" (aunt in Spanish). I told him that it sounded so beautiful to my ears. He started repeating the word a few times. As an only child, I was always concerned about not having the opportunity to feel the joy that aunts and uncles feel, and it finally happened. To this day my nephew, now an adult, sometimes calls me "tía-tía-tía-tía," and I savor the word every time.

In our house, we have a framed picture of David, my husband's little brother, who died tragically when he was almost two years old, before my husband was born. We only know David through my in-laws' stories, but he is still part of our family, and having his picture in our box is a way of acknowledging he was here. We want our kids to know about their uncle whom they never met, to see him as a real person rather than just a sad story from the past. David had an impact in the way my husband was raised and in one way or another was present in every family gathering through his parents. Now it is up to us to make sure that our family knows about David being part of the Szulik family for generations to come.

Reflect and Take Action

- How was your relationship with your sibling(s) growing up? Has it changed as you've grown older?
- Jot down five memorable stories and find five photos about your sibling(s) that you would like to share in your box.
- As a kid, did you and your siblings tease each other? Think about a particular occasion that is worth remembering.
- If you're boxing for someone else, what role did their sibling(s) play in their life?

Grandparents

I didn't find information in Charles's box about his grandparents. My box, however, includes loads of memories and items that reflect my grandparents' presence, as they played a pivotal role in my life.

I remember visiting my maternal *savta's* house on the weekends as a kid. She would let me play with her tiny wooden dolls and always had something yummy in the oven. It was always so cozy at *savta's* house, and I tried to replicate that coziness in my box with pictures of some of her gifts, recipes, and two of her tiny wooden dolls.

Teresa, a stay-at-home mom whose grandparents lived with her when she was growing up, created a photo collage of her grandparents, telling me, "It provides a good idea of their lives." She wrote down memories of celebrations with them, stories they told her that made her laugh or cry, and things she remembered them saying or doing. She is also including in her box special mementos that belonged to her grandparents, along with a picture of her grandfather's favorite hat and scarf that he wouldn't go anywhere without.

Brian, twenty-three, told me, "Since the day I was born, my grandma wrote a letter every month or two to me, and then she included my sister after she was born two years later. Her letters share a story of her life and things she wants us to know that are important to her. She told us those letters are a secret between her and us and no one can read them, not even my parents. That made it even more special, like a game. She gave me the first twelve years of letters when I was ready for it; it took me forever to read them! I never showed them to my parents because I want to honor the rules of the game my grandma established. I have stories about her growing up, stories about other relatives, stories about my mom as a child, and about things happening in the world at the time. Those letters are the first thing to go in my box without a doubt." What a gift Brian's grandma gave him and his sister. I will borrow her wonderful initiative and populate my grandchildrens' boxes with my letters.

My son and his two extraordinary grandfathers sharing their life lessons and building a strong foundation of love and wisdom.

- What are some special moments you've had with your grand-parents? Jot down some stories of memories of time together. Incorporate photos if you can.
- Are you like any of your grandparents? If so, in what way?
- Are you a grandparent, great-aunt, or great-uncle? Consider finding five pictures of your grandchildren, or grandnieces, or grandnephews, and describe them. Record yourself with messages or letters for each one of them. Describe what it means for you to be a grandparent.

Our Ancestors and the Value of Family Histories

Did you know that family narratives can be lost in three generations? I've learned that firsthand recently and I'm not surprised. I've hit a point at which my own history is vanishing right before my eyes. I want to know who my long-lost family members are. Who are the people behind the names in my family tree? How did my great-grandparents meet? My burning questions go infinitely on.

Most of us don't become interested in family history until later in life, but by then it can already be too late. Our parents or grandparents may not be alive anymore, or they might be too old to remember. We end up missing generations of family history. That gap of information is a preventable loss. To me it was always clear that the stories of my great-grandparents were my stories too, and I am saddened that I know so little about them.

Murad, a close family friend, shared, "I never got to meet my grandpa on my dad's side. Sadly, I barely know anything about him—all I know is what my dad tells me. From my other grandparents I have memories and memen-tos that I will cherish forever. I wish I knew something about the generations before. It would have been amazing to have a Box of Life that would enable me to get to know my great-grandparents." I share Murad's sentiments. I felt frustrated every time I asked my parents about our family's ancestors and they would look at me with disbelief that I assumed they had answers. And yet, it was my dad who always used to tell me, "Oriti, remember that you are who you are because others before you were who they were."

Faces of the forgotten: seeking clues in old photographs. This picture, found among my mom's family photographs, is an unsolved puzzle, reminding us of the untold tales that live within the forgotten corners of history.

My friend, Dr. Stanley Robboy, MD, who is an anatomic and clinical pathology specialist, actively tried to preserve his family history by writing a fascinating book titled *The Life and Times of John Robboy and His Mishpocha*. John Robboy was his father. The preface of the book included a sentence that resonated with me: "Remembering the past is good. Understanding it is even better."

I asked Stan what compelled him to write the book. He responded, "At its core, it answers the question 'Who am I?' The quick and easy answer is that we are the product of our parents, extended family, neighbors, and friends with whom we live now, but we are also shaped by people from generations, if not centuries, earlier. We are the embodiment of the civilization our forebearers gave us.

My fondest dream is that my book will answer the same 'Who am I?' question for my grandchildren and their grandchildren many generations from now. I hope they will say, 'Now I know who I am because I understand who my parents, siblings, cousins, and their families were.'"

Research has shown that developing a strong family narrative and knowing our family history is of great value. Among other benefits, it can:

- **Impact how we perceive ourselves.** We are a combination of the history and culture that we inherited. Our family history provides us with a sense of identity. Dr. Robyn Fivush and Natalie Merril of Emory University concluded, "Narratives of others, especially family members, become part of our own autobiography and guide our personal future . . . As others tell us their experiences, we understand our own experiences in new ways as well, using others' stories as frames."

- **Provide a sense of belonging.** It is a source of empowerment to realize that we are not alone; we are part of something greater than ourselves. Children who learn they are part of a larger narrative have a greater sense of confidence and belonging.

- **Build resilience.** From our ancestors' struggles we can learn what mistakes to avoid and from their resilience become empowered to meet challenges. We learn how they found their way through challenges, which reminds us that we can also face adversity.

- **Help us make smart health choices.** Collecting information about our family health traits, predisposition to certain disorders, and hereditary risk factors from as many generations as we can is of great benefit. This information can help us take necessary steps and make adjustments to our life-style to lower certain health risks.

- **Create meaningful bonds and emotional connections.** Our family stories connect us not only to people in our present but also our past. The more we learn about our past, the more connected we become to our ancestors and communities. It is human nature to bond with those who share our history.

- **Increase our empathy.** Learning about the hardships that those before us faced helps us understand their struggles. Personal stories create a connection that promotes understanding beyond differences. We can apply that same understanding toward others who are currently facing tough times.

- **Act as a source of truth.** Documented family stories are witnesses of cultural and social history. Familial stories work as collective memory banks.

Steve, a talented artist and woodcrafter, knows the value of capturing family history. He wrote, "My dad flew forty-one missions as navigator of a B-24 heavy bomber in WWII when he was twenty-one years old. Over my lifetime I've become more and more proud of his heroism. I have a special memento: his weathered flight bag with his name and rank stenciled on it, with forty-one little bomb insignias he'd painted on. For several years, I've been gathering as many details as I can about my dad's experiences in the United States Air Corps. I want to pass this along to my kids and other family members. I've also gathered stories about my grandparents and their siblings. They were the immigrant generation who fled a bad situation in my old country and flourished here. If I don't gather this information, nobody will enjoy the benefit of knowing about these wonderful people, our ancestors. I want others to feel the same proud feeling I have of them. I wish I'd started earlier, when I could have asked more questions and learned more. But at least in my Box of Life I can put down details I've gathered and know that it will live on."

Now it is your turn to prevent your own family from having a missing chapter in your family's life story.

Reflect and Take Action

- Next time a family member starts sharing a family story, pull your phone out and start recording!
- Collect all the information you can about your family roots and history. Start with what you know and then consult with family members, starting with the oldest. You may be surprised at how much you learn. Sometimes people don't share information unless they are asked to do so. After that you can access online resources, public records, the public library, and genealogy groups, among other resources.
- Research where family names began and how they changed over time. Through a last name you can trace history.
- Look through photos of those who came before you. (If you don't have photos ask other family members if they do.) Do some detective work and look for clues and patterns that might reveal insights and hidden information about your family.
- What five family stories do you feel responsible for preserving and passing on?

Test Your Knowledge

In 2001, Dr. Robyn Fivush and Dr. Marshall Duke developed a measure called the "Do You Know . . . ?" scale.[1] They created a list of twenty questions to ask children about their families to test the hypothesis that children who know more about their families are more resilient in the face of challenges than those who have limited knowledge about their families. I found their questions thought provoking and adapted some of them below. As you read through them, think about your own answers. Don't just respond "yes" or "no," but rather include all the information you know. You can also interview other family members. Share your answers with them and others and consider including the answers in your Box of Life.

1. Do you know where your parents met?
2. Do you know where your mother grew up? What schools did she attend?
3. Do you know where your father grew up? What schools did he attend?
4. Do you know some of the jobs that your parents had when they were young?
5. Do you know where your parents were married?
6. Do you know where your grandparents grew up?
7. Do you know where your grandparents met?
8. Do you know the source of your name?
9. Do you know which person in the family you look most like?
10. Do you know which person in the family you act most like?
11. Do you know the national background of your family (such as English, Spanish, German, Kenyan, Haitian, Russian, etc.)?
12. Do you know some of the lessons that your parents learned from good or bad experiences?

---

[1] Robyn Fivush Ph.D., "The 'Do You Know?' 20 Questions about Family Stories," *Psychology Today*, November 19, 2016, www.psychologytoday.com/us/blog/the-stories-our-lives/201611/the-do-you-know-20-questions-about-family-stories.

Our Nonhuman Family Members

If you are not a passionate animal lover like me, you might be asking yourself why I'm including our pets as family. I will defend my criteria by saying I'm not alone in considering my dog a family member. Southern Methodist University sociologist Andrea Laurent-Simpson, whose book is titled *Just Like Family: How Companion Animals Joined the Household*, reminds us that "American pet owners are transforming the cultural definition of family. Dogs and cats are treated like children, siblings, grandchildren. In fact, the American Veterinary Medical Association found that 85 percent of dog owners and 76 percent of cat owners think of their pets as family."[1]

I have had ten dogs over the course of my life (Coffee, Cofeet, Martin, Gingit, Dayan, Wanda, Sheila, Capitán, Addie, and Bubba) and have many wonderful memories of each. There was never a time they weren't happy to greet me or lie by my side. Their pictures occupy a big part of my computer's memory space, and more importantly, their paws are forever imprinted on my soul.

My friend Juana has two cats, Matilde and Demian. She shared with me that she can't imagine her life without them. She is creating a virtual Box of Life dedicated to her furry companions. It includes important vet reports, stories of special times and photographs. She is recording their sounds, filming short videos of their daily routines and favorite moments, and taking pictures of their funny facial expressions. She wants to make sure she can see them in action for as long as she is alive.

In my box, I have a timeline of all my canine family members, who have impacted me in very profound ways. I've also included a few mementos, such as a small bag with my dog Capitán's hair and my dog Dayan's birth certificate that his breeder provided to us. It saddens me that I don't know if Charles ever

---

[1] "Pets on Board: Meet the Multispecies American Family," *SMU*, July 13, 2021, www.smu.edu/News/2021/Research/Pets-on-board.

had a pet—he never mentioned one, nor did he leave any indication in his box. I do know he loved animals per his daughter, Ina. After all, as American journalist and author John Grogan says, "Such short little lives our pets have to spend with us, and they spend most of it waiting for us to come home each day."

Coffee (page 146), Capitán, Sheila, Addie, and Bubba—they are part of "My dogs' timetable" that I included in my Box of Life

Reflect and Take Action

- If you have had a nonhuman family member, share a few lines describing your friend's personality and your relationship. If you've had multiple pets, share an anecdote for each one. Try to include a picture with your stories.

> "There is no doubt that it is around the family and the home that all the greatest virtues . . . are created, strengthened, and maintained."
> —Winston Churchill

Chapter 8

Romantic Love

"I am for my beloved, and my beloved is for me."
—**King Solomon**, *Song of Songs*

Love is a powerful force that transcends time, space, and circumstance. Romantic love is a feeling that makes us feel seen, cherished, and connected. It can be tumultuous yet grounding at the same time. Love makes us all into poets. It's what we write about, what we sing about, what we dream about. For many, their romantic partner is central to their lives. And even if romance and partnership aren't currently important to us, it is very likely that we have at least one love story that impacted our lives at one point or another.

Love stories come with ups and downs, first dates and breakups, heartbreak and joy. They are cultural treasures—they tell us about the way people lived and what they valued. These stories deserve a place in your Box of Life.

Puppy Love

I've been married for thirty-two years, and yet I can still vividly recall the butterflies of my first infatuation with a boy named Roy when I was in third grade. He was just a boy in my class—not a genius or a star athlete—but to me he was the cat's meow. I think he liked me too. There's something about our first crush that makes it profoundly sweet and memorable. It's our first taste of a whole new way of relating to people. I wish I had a photo or a card or some memento from Roy to put in my box, but a few words will have to do.

By now you know that I love asking questions! I queried people about their first crush, a fun topic that we don't talk about enough. Priscila, a nurse practitioner and mother of two, told me, "I was nine years old when I had my first crush. His name was Jerome. He was a grade above me and had recently moved to my neighborhood and school. I have memories from that first crush as if it were yesterday. At first, he called me weird because I liked him. After a few months of riding the school bus together we became friends, and then, magically, my first, innocent kiss was with Jerome. We were sitting on the swings in the yard of our elementary school, and he leaned over and pecked me on the cheek. We made a lot of jokes about being boyfriend and girlfriend, but it never really happened. On Valentine's Day he gave me a box of chocolates and a tiny red teddy bear; I have a photo of them that my mom took for me because she thought it was the cutest thing, and that, along with a few other memories, is going into my box. When we started middle school, Jerome moved and I lost track of him. But I don't think I'll ever forget him."

Jacobo, a lab technician about to get married, shared, "A strange and wonderful thing happened the other day. I was packing my stuff to move in with my soon-to-be wife, and I found a memento that I'd forgotten about—an old shin guard from my high school recreational soccer-playing days. It triggered memories of a girl I met my junior year. We were on the same coed soccer team, and there was something about her that made all the other girls around her fade away. I remember how hard I tried to impress her. One day, after winning an important game, she gave me a hug—that day was one of the happiest days of my life. I kept the shin guard I wore that day. When Kathy hugged me, it was a boost for my self-esteem and perhaps the confidence I needed to start dating."

Do you remember your first crush? Can you conjure the feelings? How might you commemorate these in your box?

First True Love

Our first everything is always memorable. Our first kiss, our first car, our first trophy, and our first loss will likely be vividly remembered. But our first love may play an extra-special role in our lives. It is the gate that opens a whole new way of feeling and connecting with another human being. Through our first love we discover how we can care about someone else in ways we didn't know were possible. For many of us, that first love remains with us forever, even if we were the ones to end it and are completely over it.

I believe Charles's first love was Mildred, his wife. For me it was Gaby, my husband. I've dated and had my dose of heartbreaks, but with Gaby I discovered what *love* really meant to me. When you fall in love with someone, it is easy to get swept up in the excitement of it all. But when it comes time to move beyond this initial phase, it's important to look at your relationship through a grounding lens. What do you really want out of your relationship? What are you willing to compromise? What do you need from each other? What do you need from yourself? These are all questions worth asking ourselves, and the answers might be reflected in our boxes.

My first date, first kiss, first boyfriend (who was not necessarily my first love), my first heartbreak, first love letter . . . I cherish them all, and they all play a role in my box. I have letters, photos, and journal entries that bring the relationships to light and attest to their impact on my life. I won't indulge you with those stories, but I will say all these firsts were worth it, despite the tears they might have drawn.

Would you agree?

From young hearts in 1986 to a lifelong story, our journey together began with that special spark at the age of nineteen.

> *"Every great love starts with a great story."*
> —Nicholas Sparks, *The Notebook*

Reflect and Take Action

- Create a timetable of your romantic firsts—first crush, first kiss, first heartbreak, first true love.
- What roles do love and affection play in your life?
- Looking at your relationships throughout your life, do you notice any patterns or tendencies in your behavior or the people involved? Do you have a "type"?
- If you're boxing for someone else, be sure to include their romantic relationships. Look through old letters and photos and see what you can find.

When Charles Met Mildred

Love stories are beautiful. They reveal so much about other people's values, priorities, and personality traits. Yet we usually don't know the details of the love stories of even the people closest to us. In fact, one of my favorite questions to ask couples is how they met. It always makes me smile to see their faces light up as they go back in time to that special moment.

During one of our talks, I asked Charles to tell me how he met his Mildred. He happily agreed, but rather than launch right in at that moment, he said he would tell me later, almost as if he needed time to think it over to make sure he didn't miss any details. I could tell how important this story was to him. A few days later, what seemed like a novella arrived in my inbox. It was from Charles. He asked me to share the story of how he and the love of his life came together, and I'm honored to fulfill his wish:

"Everything I had experienced in my life was mundane, until I met my Mildred. It was an awakening. Mildred was a kindergarten teacher, and I was trying to find a place for myself in broadcasting and theater while attending college at night. The school at which Mildred taught produced an annual parent-teacher play, and Mildred was involved. In their search for a director, a parent volunteer who was also a friend of mine suggested I fill the role. I gladly accepted. It would prove to be the best decision I ever made.

The first meeting was held in the home of one of the actors. There, I met Mildred. I was opinionated as much then as I am now, and so was she. Unsurprisingly, we took an instant dislike to each other. However, as time passed, we began to respect each other's opinions and even became friends. The play was successful, and our friendship grew closer, even though I was dating other people. To put it simply, we enjoyed each other's company but never seriously considered a romantic involvement. Things had been this way for about a year.

As an actor, I was often cast in radio shows. On the way to one rehearsal, I was running late but stopped for something to eat. After I dashed out of the restaurant, I turned left and fell down into a basement. Many buildings in New York City have openings that require a bar to hold the doors open to prevent a fall. The bar on these doors was not in place. My back was hurt, and I was taken to the hospital. Winter had arrived full blast, which prevented my family from visiting me. During the worst part of the storm, the

Charles and Mildred on their wedding day

door to my hospital room opened, and I saw the most welcome sight: Mildred, smiling in the doorway, even though on the way to see me, she had slipped and hurt her back too! Mildred was the only person to brave the storm—and her own pain as well—and in that moment I decided that she was the woman for me. We were married on July 4, 1948."

Of all the things I found in Charles's box, the ones that touched me the most were the love poems written by Mildred to Charles on Valentine's Days and their anniversaries. Handwritten on paper that was now yellowed, wrinkled, and worn out, these poems all attested to their deep connection and lasting love. Mildred signed most of the poems "Your Mildred." Reading them, I felt like I was watching the movie *The Notebook* over and over again.

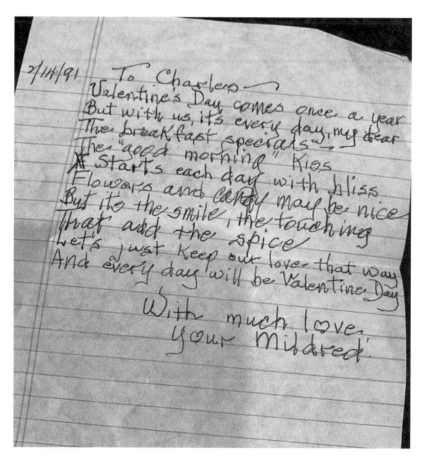

In awe I watch you--so filled with wonder and excitement,
Not unlike an inquisitive child,
So eager to learn, to delve into the unknown,
To ferret out the secrets of the Universe.

You've enriched my life in so many ways...
Art, music, theater, books give us food for conversations,
With meaning and depth.
New people and places add new horizons to daily living.

You're so young in spirit, in action, in thought...
I'm so pleased that you've taken me along
On your never-ending quest for life and its meaning and its joys.

Your foray into sculpture, just 8 years ago,
Started as a hobby, a way to pass the time,
Now it is all-consuming and a totally involving quest,
With study, writing, speaking, teaching...
An opportunity to reach out, to convey
Richness, meaning and beauty to the people you meet

What a joy it is to see the light in your eyes,
As you set out to speak, or teach, or read a new book
In your growing library of stimulating and enlightening writings.

May you enjoy abundant good health,
May you continue to enjoy your out-reaching pursuits,
May you continue to inspire those whom you meet,
May our journey, together, continue for many years to come.

With much love,

Mildred

Charles inspired me to make sure my own love story is never lost in time, so I have written down the story of how I met Gaby—my husband now for thirty-two years—and it's also in my box, front and center.

When Orit Met Gaby

It was 1986 in the beautiful city of Buenos Aires, Argentina, and I was nineteen years old. My friend Cynthia called me to ask if I had plans for the weekend, as her boyfriend's best friend, who was studying at Hebrew University in Jerusalem, was home visiting his family. His name was Gabriel (Gaby).

As soon as I saw Gaby, I remembered that I had encountered him two years earlier. I had been in Israel visiting friends, riding a tour bus on our way to a snowy Jerusalem. I had noticed him interacting with other people and immediately liked him, but he didn't even notice me. Two years later, here we were. Our paths were meant to cross again, and life made sure of it.

Cynthia, Silvio, Gaby, and I went to an amusement park in the middle of Buenos Aires called the Italpark. I was not a big fan of amusement parks, but I was determined to challenge my fears and step out of my comfort zone. I'd only ridden a roller coaster at Italpark once before a few years earlier, and I did it hoping the boy I liked would hold my hand. It worked. I knew this night might be the second time I would experience a roller coaster while holding a boy's hand. I was right.

I've always been a clumsy person. I struggle to dance in rhythm or catch a fast ball. But that night—oh, my—I was winning every arcade game we played, throwing balls and hitting every target. I was unstoppable. I was on fire. Ever since that night, I believe in divine intervention!

After the amusement park and a fun dinner, we went back to my apartment, where my parents were already sleeping. In Buenos Aires, most college students live with their parents, and I was no exception. Standing in the kitchen before saying goodbye, Gaby very politely asked if he could see me again that week. Right after he and our friends left at 3:00 a.m., I walked into my parents' room. Gently, I woke my mom up and I told her, "Ima, I met my future husband." Barely opening her eyes, she whispered, "Go to sleep." I smiled and left the room. I knew it. I felt it in my bones.

The entire week had nearly gone by, and Gaby still hadn't called. It was Friday night and I had to leave for work—I was a leader at a Jewish Youth Movement. Instead of wearing my usual sneakers and jeans, I pulled something nicer together. I told my mom I had a feeling Gaby would be waiting for me when I was done; she thought I was fooling myself. But I was right. And that's how our story started.

Gaby decided to finish his college degree in Buenos Aires instead of returning to Hebrew University. We started seeing each other more often. At one point, we took a nine-month break from one another, but all in all, we dated for about five years before deciding to get married. Thirty-two years later, we are still happily married.

If you ask Gaby whether he knew I was his future wife when he first saw me, he would say no, and I believe him. But it doesn't matter, because one of us knew, and that's enough. And, of course, what's really important is the ongoing relationship. Take Charles and Mildred—they started out disliking each other and look how well they turned out. Love stories come in many shapes and forms. What binds them together is how much joy they can bring.

Gabriel and me on our wedding day, August 4, 1991

- If you are in a relationship, how did you meet your spouse or partner? When did you know they were the person for you?
- On paper or recording, share what impressed you about your partner while you were dating.
- What have you learned or discovered with your partner about love? What would you want to share on the topic with younger generations?

When Nathalie Met Harold

I love hearing people's love stories, not only because they are often so joyous but also because they prove we never know what may be waiting for us right around the corner. It also doesn't hurt that people usually look so happy when they're telling them. My friend Nathalie was a case in point—she lit up while she shared the tale of how she and her late husband Harold came together:

"When I was in college in 1947, Harold was dating one of my sorority sisters, so I knew who he was. They broke up and I left college never giving him another thought. I was twenty-one and returned home to Atlanta after graduating in 1950, and I began teaching the second grade that fall. My friend Barbara had a suitor, Stuart, who lived in Macon, Georgia, and desperately wanted to woo her. She, on the other hand, was enamored with someone else. Nonetheless, Stuart called to make a date with Barbara. She accepted on the condition that I would come along. Stuart asked his friend Harold, who lived in an adjoining small town, Milledgeville, to be my date, and he accepted. And so, the story continued.

In those days, stores in small towns closed on Wednesday afternoons. So, every Wednesday (and soon following, every weekend), Harold would drive up to be with me. This was 1950. There was no interstate, mostly just two-lane roads and mostly in poor repair. It is amazing that he did not get killed on those dark nights returning to Milledgeville.

During that Christmas holiday, I went to a convention in Atlantic City, and teasing him, I told him I would let him know if I wanted to continue seeing him or not. Well, when I returned home, he read me the riot act. He asked me to make up my mind if I wanted to keep seeing him or not! I did, and he continued to drive up to be with me. One evening, we were sitting in front of the fireplace in my parents' living room, and he asked me to marry him. Now, he was a wonderful, kind, caring, loving person, and I knew he cared deeply for me, so I said yes! He told me later that on the way home he thought, "What have I just done?" The ladies who worked for him in his store said he would sit in the back of the store and just smile. In February, my parents came to visit Harold's parents and brought a ring he had arranged to purchase. That afternoon he gave me the ring, and we were married June 24, 1951. Through thick and thin, we were married almost sixty-one years and had three children—two boys, Robert and Michael, and a girl, Beth. They were amazing kids. We were married sixty years when Harold was diagnosed with inoperable pancreatic cancer. He died March 21, 2011. So that life ended and a new, single one began."

The death of a life partner is a profound loss, creating a deep void. Even cherished memories of good times together can be sad, because they remind you of what you've lost. But there are ways you can revisit those memories without succumbing to a flood of sorrow. We do that by asking questions that guide our memories to revisit moments of joy and accomplishments we shared with our deceased

Harold and Nathalie

partner. That's how I coached Nathalie while she put together her box. We found ourselves laughing about many of her memories with Harold. We gathered photos of the two of them together and wrote down stories of moments they shared. These photos triggered memories Nathalie had long forgotten and brought her a lot of joy.

Lasting Love

Mildred's poems to Charles, Nathalie's reminiscences of Harold, and my parents' sixty-one-year marriage share characteristics of long, healthy relationships. From my own research and from observing couples who lasted and those who didn't, I believe certain aspects tend to be present in those who have healthy marriages:

- Their communications are honest and open; they talk, talk, and talk!
- They mutually respect, admire, and trust each other.
- They share values.
- They have a solid support system of family and friends.
- They never stop dating each other; they have moments of romance, seduction, sexual attraction, and playfulness. They know that "love" is an active verb.
- They remember what made them fall in love in the first place.
- They embrace new experiences and new projects as a couple.
- Their coupledom never takes away from their individual independence; they value self-actualization and personal fulfillment.
- They are good companions to each other.
- They share a spirit of fun.

As I said, these are based on personal observation. What have you observed about successful relationships? What do you think are the characteristics of a long-term commitment to another person? If you wanted to convey the foundation of your relationship in your box, how would you capture it?

Heartbreaks

Some relationships don't work out exactly how we thought they would. Sometimes our expectations are smashed against the rocks of reality. Painful as they are, heartbreaks are memorable too. The sorrow, disappointment, and frustration can linger for years. It implies a previous commitment that someone broke without

This photo is in my dad's box: my parents on their honeymoon in Venice, Italy.

our permission. Walking away from what you thought was special leaves a bitter taste that is hard to forget. Fortunately, time is a good healer.

I still remember my first broken heart. It happened when I was sixteen, and my boyfriend dumped me for another girl. My mom was so worried by my extreme sadness, she sent me to therapy. My therapist's advice was, "First, take some time to grieve. Let yourself cry and feel the pain of the loss before trying to move on with life again. Then start rebuilding your self-esteem by thinking about all the things you've accomplished so far, all the people that love you, and all the goals you always shared with me that you want to accomplish. Think how much better things will be when you're dating someone else who appreciates all the qualities in you!" For me it was hard to think there would ever be another love in my life, but of course there was.

Samantha, a teacher who is starting her Box of Life, shared, "It was a simple breakup. We were in a long-distance relationship, dating for almost two years. He made other plans for the weekend that we were supposed to spend together. I didn't have a lot of time to think about it—I just knew that I felt like someone had died. I remember sitting on my bedroom floor, surrounded by all the things he'd given me: his favorite shirt, which smelled like him; a rope bracelet he won at an arcade for me; and little notes he'd written me when we were apart. I took each one and held it close to my heart, crying as if the world were to end. Now I'm stuffing some of his notes into my Box of Life. One day they will remind me of the things I've learned from that painful experience. And they'll also remind me of all the great people who do love me no matter what."

In cases of heartbreak, our boxes serve much like a therapeutic hope box—as a reminder of why our life is precious. A hope box consists of a collection of items that show that our life is meaningful and worth living. This is a technique often used in cognitive behavioral therapy (CBT). In our Box of Life, alongside mementos of heartbreak, we will have items that remind us that we are loved and that life will keep us moving forward. We will have letters, cards, and emails from those who care about us, pictures that conjure positive memories (of family, friends, vacations, etc.), documentation of accomplishments (report cards, diplomas, certificates, awards, etc.), art that someone has made for us, along with many other things. Hopefully we will also have mementos of our next love story, to which we will arrive with greater wisdom and renewed dreams.

But even if love doesn't turn out exactly how we hoped it would—even if our expectations don't match up with reality—there is still so much beauty in this world that can only be found when we open up to love again—and again, and again!

Reflect and Take Action

- What are five characteristics that you believe are present in those who have fulfilling, healthy, long relationships? This is a good topic of discussion with others as well.

- Were you ever heartbroken? Did you ever break someone else's heart? Share the stories.

Curating Our Love Stories

Many of us hold on to quite a few keepsakes from our relationships in general, and from our wedding in particular. For example, I have two heavy photo albums with hundreds of wedding photos, my wedding dress, videos, gift lists, all the greetings, cards, and telegrams we received, and more. In my box, however, I only have ten photos, our wedding invitation, and the videos of our ceremony and party. Putting together our Box of Life is an opportunity to select the most meaningful, essential items—the ones that represent the whole story.

Here are a few ideas:

- Select just ten wedding-related photos for your box—make it clear why these ten are so special.
- Jot down your memories of the wedding. What were the highlights? Did anything go wrong?
- Include a guest list if you had one. It's amazing what you forget and how friendships change. You may be surprised twenty years later by who was there and who was not.
- Consider leaving it at that. Of course, if there's something else you must include, add it—but remember, less can be more.

Love Stories from the Past

There's something deeply satisfying about knowing our ancestors' love stories. It may be partially because love stories are universal and eternal. But it also may be because it gives us a window to our own origins.

Of course, with old family stories, we never really know what's true and what's not, but it doesn't matter—so long as we understand their essence. The beauty of preserving these tales goes beyond fact-checking. Throughout history, the most powerful stories have been those that chronicle love and human relationships.

Natalia, one of my high-school best friends once told me, "I have a torn piece of paper written in pen by my paternal grandmother. It reads that she wants to be buried next to her husband. Her husband, my grandfather, died at a very young age, fifty years before she did. I don't know their story well, only that she bragged that she won him over while she was collecting fruits from a tree on top of a ladder. From below, my grandfather could see her ankles and she considered that naughty. That torn paper was stored by my mom in her house, and I now have it in my safe."

Steve Goldberg, a teacher and historian, once told me, "My grandmother told me a story about how her mother was married to her father and he had come over to Canada before her. She was scheduled to come to the United States on a ship, but it was Queen Victoria's Diamond Jubilee celebration, and she had the opportunity to see it, so she took a later ship and didn't tell anyone. The ship she was supposed to be on sunk, and her husband mourned her death. When she showed up a few weeks later, nobody was there to meet her, which annoyed her. She took a carriage to her husband's house, and when she got there, he almost fainted because he thought she was dead and he was seeing a ghost. No idea if that's true. I wish I knew more."

Gerry Garbulsky, the director of TED en Español, writes a weekly newsletter that I never skip called "Ideas Para Empezar La Semana" (Ideas to Start the Week). He recently shared a family story in his newsletter that I found enlightening. Gerry was happy to permit me to share his story with you. This is *Mi Tatarabuela y el Tétano* (My Great-Great-Grandmother and the Tetanus):

My great-great-grandmother (on my mom's side) was born sometime between 1855 and 1860 and raised in a town in Romania. She married at a very young age, around sixteen years old. We have no idea if she was in love—if that was even something they asked themselves back then—or was forced into it.

We don't know what her husband did for a career, but we know she would wait for him at home all day, spending most of her time knitting. One day she set her knitting materials down on a chair and went to grab a drink from the kitchen. In that moment, her husband walked through the front door, returning from a long day at work. Tired, he sunk into the chair, thinking he could finally rest. Instead, he had such bad luck that he accidentally sat directly on top of the knitting needle she had left there, and it went straight up his—well, you can use your imagination.

It turns out the knitting needle was rusty and dirty, because my great-great-grandmother's husband became infected with tetanus and died a short time later.

At just the age of nineteen, she was a widow. Becoming a widow at such a young age was not well perceived, and she had no choice but to comply with quickly remarrying, this time to a man thirty years older than her. With that man, my great-great-grandfather, they birthed twelve children. The youngest of the twelve was Rebeca, my great-grandmother, who arrived in Buenos Aires in 1905, and whom I had the chance to know.

I was told this story for the first time by my grandmother, Rebeca's daughter, when I was just a child. This story had a big impact on me and generated contradictory feelings every time I got the tetanus shot—on one hand, I'm thankful to be protected from the infection; on another hand, I owe my life to tetanus. If it hadn't been for my great-great-grandmother's first husband's infection, I may never have been born.

Gerry's story is not necessarily romantic but is a great example of a short story that illuminates more about our families' pasts—specifically in the context of romance, relationships, and "how it all began."

Reflect and Take Action

- Do you know how your great-great-grandparents met? What about your grandparents? If you do, it is time to document whatever you know. If you don't, try and find out any information you can. The longer you wait, the less likely those family stories will be preserved.

"Love is not breathlessness, it is not excitement, it is not the promulgation of promises of eternal passion. That is just being 'in love,' which any fool can do. Love itself is what is left over when being in love has burned away, and it is both an art and a fortunate accident. Those that truly love have roots that grow toward each other underground, and when all the pretty blossoms have fallen from their branches, they find that they are one tree and not two."
—from *Captain Corelli's Mandolin* by Louis de Bernières, excerpt found in Charles's box

Chapter 9

Friendship

"He who seeks perfection in a friend will stay without friends."

—**Yiddish proverb**

My *savta* used to tell me that you can learn a lot about people based on who their friends are. "You are who you spend time with. Those are the people who will determine who you will become," she would always say. Like my grandmother, I'm a strong believer that our friends—as much as our family—make us who we are and who we are not. They influence us for better and for worse. In time we begin to act like our friends, often without realizing it. But if we're careful about the friends we choose and how they treat us, they can even challenge us and make us better people than we were before we met them.

Of course, we have many different kinds of friends. I have a few friends who I consider "soul" friends. I also have a few eternal friends rooted in my childhood—these relationships are unconditional and surpass any distance. I have close friends who feel like extended family and others who I am not so close with, but I would still consider them friends. I have many wonderful acquaintances, some who I see often, and some nearly never. In the real world, friendship is not defined by how often you talk to or see someone. It is rather defined by the underlying bond and a unique, heartfelt connection that transcends the superficialities of life, time, and space.

Science has proven that friends are perhaps the most effective health insurance we have. In fact, multiple studies suggest that the effect of social connections on our life span is twice as strong as that of exercising and the equivalent to quitting smoking. We humans are social creatures and need connection. Alongside family bonds and romantic relationships, friendship provides that connection. Lydia Denworth, an award-winning science writer and author of *Friendship: The Evolution, Biology, and Extraordinary Power of Life's Fundamental Bond*, explains, "A friendship is an organism that shifts its shape across our life spans according to our abilities and availability—in other words, according to how much we open ourselves to possibilities. While there is a natural variation in our taste and need for companionship, there are some universals in what draws us together or throws us apart. And there is a bottom line—a biological need for connection that must be met to achieve basic health and well-being."[1]

What We Look for in Our Friends

Out of nowhere, Charles once asked me, "Orit, who are your friends? Describe them to me." I remember answering by sharing my "friend criteria."

First and foremost, I try to surround myself with optimistic people. My friends are active listeners and have curious minds. They are not turbulent in their souls or demanding in their nature. For my best friends, I gravitate toward people who challenge me to keep growing, who are empathetic and compassionate human beings, and who don't hold grudges. My friends are lifelong learners who inspire me to be one myself. My friends never tell me they're too busy when I need them most. My friends know how to ask for and offer help. My friends can be trusted with my eyes closed. My friends

---

[1]   Article without source that was shared with me. More about Lydia Denworth at https://lydiadenworth.com.

show their vulnerabilities and embrace mine. My friends can disagree with me and yet still respectfully and genuinely listen to everyone's voices. My friends can help me identify my blind spots and are appreciative when I point out theirs.

I asked a few of my friends for their definition of friendship. The most beautiful one came from my friend Gaby, who wrote, "Friendship is a feeling that connects people . . . with an unwavering passion. Friends don't expect anything from each other . . . [T]hey enjoy being with each other. A friend is our continuity, our extension. A friendship that was born in childhood or youth can't be killed by anyone, not even by death itself!"

I found an excerpt from an article in Charles's box that speaks to his conception of friendship: "Becoming a friend takes practice. Friends help you overcome loneliness and add joy to living. A true friend is a person who recognizes your faults and overlooks them." He often mentioned his friends to me, and his box reflects his ability to easily connect with people. Among other things it includes numerous notes that others had sent him, expressing their love and admiration, as well as articles that he wrote in which he mentions people with whom he had meaningful conversations.

"I broke bread with Sol," he once said with excitement. "Who is Sol?" I asked. Charles enthusiastically told me about his new friend and their projects together. He explained, "You make friends as you go, and it keeps you going because you always know there are more to come." I was lucky to witness how his friendship with Sol developed. At times they were like two adult kids on a playground, sharing their dreams and hopes for the future, and, as anyone else who became close to Charles did, working on projects together.

Charles spoke to people's values and their interests. He could be very critical because he had high expectations that were hard to meet, yet when he cared for someone, he cared deeply for them.

Reflect and Take Action

- What does friendship mean to you?
- What five things do you treasure most about your friends?
- What did you like to do with your friends during different stages of your life?
- Have you ever taken a stand against what your friends wanted you to do? Share the experience.
- What are three things that you learned from your friends, and how would you be different if you hadn't met them?
- If you are boxing for your children, consider including a photo of your child and their best friend doing something together that they enjoy. You can create a friendship timeline, adding a few photos every year. If you are boxing for yourself, you can do the same thing!
- If you are boxing for a parent or a loved one, consider creating a friendship timeline for them—or at least some stories about their friendships. You might need to do some detective work, but the stories that you will uncover might well be worth the effort.

Virtual Friends

It's a shame that social media took off during one of Charles's later stages in life. I often imagine how much joy he would have found in connecting with thousands of people and sharing his ideas online. We both agreed that connections are what keep the world spinning!

As a "nomad" who moved from country to country, social media has been a game changer for me. It has allowed me to bring people from different corners of the world and various stages of my life into one place. Sharing my experiences with others and learning about what others are experiencing both make my life richer. I've been able to connect with old friends while also keeping up with the news and trends in my industry. It's made me feel like part of a community and also helps me stay connected with people who are doing amazing work around the world.

But real friendship is much more than being connected online. Real friendship involves one-on-one or small-group communication—ideally getting together in person, but if not, then talking on the phone, video chatting, emailing, or texting. With real friends you know the nuances of their facial expressions and vocal tones. You know what's important to them and who they care about. There's room in our lives for online "friends" for sure, but in real life, friends are invaluable.

Commemorating Friendship in Our Boxes

Many of us make friends throughout our lifetimes—we befriend our colleagues, our neighbors, the other parents at our kids' schools, and more. These friendships can be deeply satisfying. But perhaps for the same reason that our teenage and early adult memories are so vivid, many of us have strong feelings about and deep connections to the friends we made as teenagers and young adults. I know that my high school friends left me with memories that are warm, joyful, and eternal. In my box I have a few notes I got from my friends for *El Día del Amigo* (Friendship Day), which is celebrated in Argentina on July 20, and pictures from the overnight camps that we attended, among other things. When I asked my friend Gaby what he would put in his box, he said without hesitation it would be the photo of a 110-line bus that we used to take every time we would go out. I loved this response and told him I would add the picture of Imperio, the pizza place where we would always meet at the corner of Canning and Corrientes in the neighborhood of Villa Crespo.

My friend Isabel has written a best-friends timeline for her box, including photos and a few sentences about what she loves best about each pal. And, inspired by her box of life, Ramona wrote a letter to each of her closest friends, recalling favorite memories and sharing her affection and admiration for them.

Forever bonded: chronicles of youth and friendship. In the embrace of laughter and shared adventures, Miguel Z"L, Héctor, Gaby, Sandra, and myself, weave a timeless tale of friendship that stands strong against the test of years.

Reflect and Take Action

- Reach out to friends from your past and share your memories—they might have many more memories to share with you.
- Create a friendship timeline. What similarities do you see

among your friends across your lifetime? What differences?

- Include your best friends' names, contact information, and any other information you can provide about them and their families in case someone in your family one day wants to track them down. Remember, it is a small world we live in!

My Friendship with Charles

There was a forty-plus-year age difference between Charles and me, but our friendship transcended that gap. Call it chemistry or friendship at first sight, but from the moment we met, we liked each other. In a *Psychology Today* article titled "Why We Click with Our Best Friends Right from the Start," Suzanne Degges-White, PhD writes, "We [also] sometimes experience the near-magical phenomenon of moving from strangers to best friends in almost no time at all. I call it the 'click phenomenon.'"[1] Charles and I had that click phenomenon. We had so much in common and enjoyed each other's company. I always considered Charles a friend, not an "older friend."

When he called, I answered, and when he just showed up, I made time to see him. The one day that I was over-whelmed with deadlines and chose to avoid Charles, closing the doors of my office when I heard his inimitable voice in the hall, he and Mildred were in a car accident. My recollection is that he suffered a heart attack while driving. When I went to visit them at the hospital, I felt ashamed and made a commitment to never avoid anyone who is important to me ever again. Fortunately, Charles and Mildred recovered, and

Me and Charles behind his majestic desk. This is the only photo we have together.

---

1   Degges-White Ph.D., Suzanne. "Why We Click With Our Best Friends Right From the Start." *Psychology Today*, 17 Sept. 2014, https://www.psychologytoday.com/us/blog/lifetime-connections/201409/why-we-click-our-best-friends-right-the-start.

that incident became, as Charles put it, just another story to tell.

He would often tell me, "Slow down Orit. You are speaking too quickly and with your accent it makes it hard to understand," which was what my parents always told me, even when I was speaking in my native language, Spanish. They referred not only to how fast I speak, but also to how fast I engage, react, or make sure everything is taken care of. I would always respond to their complaint by explaining, "If I slow down, I stop being me. I'm passionate, and without passion, I can't live." I would never say that to Charles. Instead, I would listen, and when I wouldn't slow down, he would make me repeat the same sentence over and over again until it was clear.

He started to get very comfortable with me, to the point that he once told me, "Nice, you gained some weight. It looks good," complimenting me like my grandmother would do. She always wanted me to gain weight as a sign of good health. Charles and my *savta* are the only ones who could tell me that and I would take it as a compliment! When my dad told me the same thing, I didn't take it so well and immediately went on a diet. I simply assigned a different meaning to his words.

Charles was a true friend. We both benefited from what we each brought to the relationship, which was no doubt enriched by our age difference. We could speak for hours about everything. We held different perspectives on *many* issues. Often our debates ended with our agreement that we were both right, not just because we loved to be right but also because, as Charles always said with an understanding yet resigned tone, "Times have changed." Each perspective was right for its time.

Being Charles's friend provided me with a much more positive attitude toward aging and gave Charles more opportunities to visit his youth. He offered me the wisdom of what matters most in the long run. He gave me

"The best thing to hold onto in life is each other."
—Audrey Hepburn

the gift of understanding that you can always have dreams, projects, and youth in your soul, no matter how old you are in physical years. I could see in Charles's spirit what novelist Madeleine L'Engle beautifully said: "The great thing about getting older is that you don't lose all the other ages you've been."

The Gifts of Intergenerational Friendships

You may have heard of the "generation gap," in which people of different generations don't understand each other or share the same interests. Intergenerational friendships can bridge that gap! They are a great way to learn about new things and gain new perspectives. You get to see how another generation—older or younger—thinks about various issues, and you can learn about concerns you might not have considered before.

A beautiful intergenerational story that touched me deeply is one between Steve Goldberg, who is a veteran high school teacher, Holocaust educator, and lawyer in his forties, and Abe Piasek, an elderly Holocaust survivor. Steve wrote, "When I first met my friend Abe Piasek, he had just turned ninety. He came to my school as a Holocaust survivor speaker. I knew nothing about him . . . so the weekend before I met him, I googled 'Abe Piasek' and ended up watching five to six hours of his speeches online. I had found a part of Abe's digital Box of Life. He had a powerful story of survival as he was taken from his family in Poland at the age of thirteen. He toiled at three slave labor camps from 1942–45. When he was liberated in 1945 at age sixteen, Abe weighed eighty pounds. Once we met, I followed up and interviewed him at his house in Raleigh, North Carolina, to learn more about his life. We became good friends.

Just as our friendship was growing, Abe fell in his garage. Three days before he died, Abe asked me to keep telling his story. I am fulfilling his wish through a project called "My Friend, Abe" (www.myfriendabe.com). About six months after his funeral, Abe's daughter Pam was going through all of Abe's things in his house, and she set aside three "boxes for Steve" filled with items of Abe's that she thought I could use to keep his story alive. I am glad I know so much about Abe's story and for our friendship, but I also wish Abe himself had taken the time to organize his own Box of Life. I think I've captured the essence of Abe, but I do wish I'd met him a few years earlier and had more time to help him build his box to include more than just his life during the Holocaust (though those six years from 1939–45 could fill several boxes of their own)." As Steve builds his own Box of Life, his friendship with Abe will make an appearance. Both lives, Steve's and Abe's, were enhanced by their friendship.

Reflect and Take Action

- If you don't have an intergenerational friendship, I encourage you to develop one. You can start by looking at your own relatives. Is there someone older or younger than you whom you'd like to get to know better? Make a date and spend some time learning about their life and ideals.

"A friendship that can end never really began."
　　　—Publilius Syrus

Chapter 10

Mentors and Teachers

"We learn something from everyone who passes through our lives. Some lessons are painful, some are painless . . . but all are priceless."

–Unknown

O ur Boxes of Life would not be complete without tributes to our mentors, teachers, and other guides who played impactful roles in making us who we are. For many of us, our parents head the list of our mentors and teachers. For others, it is about those we met in formal or informal educational settings: bosses, camp counselors, coworkers, friends, celebrities, or even strangers who were unaware that their actions or words changed someone's life. For example, my college counselor made a passing remark, recommending that I "choose the professor and not just the class." This small piece of advice made a huge difference in my college experience. In my box I've included a notebook with the best advice I've received over the years, and my college counselor's tidbit is included. I'm still adding the words of wisdom of others as years go by.

Charles's Mentors

In Charles's box, one person who appeared several times was his rabbi, Samuel Stahl, who led the temple Charles attended in San Antonio for twenty-six years. I found letters from Rabbi Stahl to Charles, a photo of Stahl, and brochures they had created together for community programs. Rabbi Stahl was deeply committed to enhancing interfaith relations through programs that promote dialogue and understanding. When Charles moved to our community in North Carolina, he continued what he had learned from Rabbi Stahl and became an integral part of the Jewish Federation's Community Relations Council. There is no better way to honor a mentor than to take what they have taught us and put it into practice.

Mentors and teachers can also be people we've never even met. At the top of this list for Charles was Dr. Martin Luther King Jr. Charles was inspired by MLK's determination, vision, and courage to stand for what he believed was right, even in the face of opposition. Charles always strived to be a leader, and MLK was his blueprint. On Martin Luther King Jr. Day, Charles organized and led programs to honor MLK's teachings.

Reflect and Take Action

- Who are the people who have inspired you to become a better version of yourself? Think about your teachers, coaches, therapists, bosses, friends, family members, neighbors, coworkers, authors, spiritual figures, fictional characters, and even strangers who said something, perhaps even only in passing, that left a mark in you.
- How are you honoring their teachings?
- Are you a teacher or mentor for someone else? If so, in which ways?

Those Who Taught Me

I've been fortunate to have many wonderful mentors and teachers over the course of my life. Their support and encouragement were invaluable in empowering me to pursue my dreams, and their wisdom and guidance shaped me into who I am. I'm proud to commemorate them in my box, keeping their wisdom close at hand so that I can continue to draw upon their insights as I move forward in life.

Here are a few examples of mentors and teachers who are celebrated in my box:

- **My dad (Shmuel Aviram Ramler):** My father is my role model. It is from observing him and how he lived his life that I developed my core values and passion for community work. As an international emissary and diplomat, he also taught me that the world is connected and that any geographic or cultural differences can be overcome by our shared humanity. In my box I have my dad's life story, his first photo with me as an infant, another one of him holding me when I took my first step, and a letter he wrote to me when I turned fifty.

- **Gustavo Perednik:** Gustavo is an Argentinean-born Israeli author, educator, rabbi, and spiritual leader. He founded a Jewish education center and youth movement that I participated in during my teenage years. Among many other teachings, Gustavo used to say, "We are always halfway." This quote is in my box; to me it means understanding that we must be satisfied with where we are and remember that there is still more work to be done. It's not about seeking perfection or completion, which don't exist. It's about honoring your accomplishments while recognizing that there is always more to learn, do, give, and become. Think about it in your own life for a few minutes: What else could you be learning? Doing? Giving? Becoming? Just like Charles, Gustavo always believed in me, more than I believed in myself, offering me opportunities to do important work within the organization that advanced not only my career but also my self-esteem. I now try to take a similar approach with young people in whom I see great potential.

- **Lila Artusi:** Lila was my high school biology teacher. She revealed to me that the right teacher could make any subject interesting and fun. She had a warm smile that made an intimidating subject like biology friendly and approachable. She also truly cared about her students' well-being beyond just schoolwork. She knew who we were as people. To this day, almost forty-five years later, we keep in touch over social media. Lila influenced my teaching style and my love for learning, and I commemorated her in my box with a paragraph I wrote that covers what I admire about her.

- **My grandmother (Shoshana Ramler):** My grandmother passed away many years before I was born. However, I've always had a picture of her in my office, and it will go in my box. It's of her working the swamps in the early days of Israel. From the many stories I've been told, I know my grandmother was a visionary who stood for causes and actively worked with people to achieve them, rather than sitting on the sidelines. Despite the fact I never met her, these are traits that I always try to emulate.

My grandmother, Shoshana Ramler, working the swamps around 1910 in the early days of the State of Israel before the British Mandate

- **Rabbi Steven G. Sager Z"L (of blessed memory):**
  He was director of Sicha, and Rabbi Emeritus of Beth El
  Synagogue in Durham, NC, where he served as a rabbi for
  thirty-two years. Since the day I moved to the United States,
  he has been my teacher, rabbinic adviser, and mentor on so
  many occasions. He was also my "fellow traveler" (as he called
  it) during my goodbye to my dad, bringing meaning and even
  beauty to a difficult journey. Whenever I was struggling to
  work through a difficult situation, I turned to Rabbi Sager.
  With his wisdom and calming, reassuring voice, he helped
  me interpret any occasion by asking the right questions and
  citing beautiful biblical sources, poems, and literature. One
  of his poems is in my box. His teachings serve as a compass
  for navigating life, and I will always miss our conversations.

Thinking about how impactful my own mentors were made me curious
about who influenced my teachers and mentors and whether they still reference their teachings. Rabbi Sager's response was a gift. Everything he wrote
helped me better understand not only what he valued but also about his
essence formula—my theory that just as a perfume is created by selecting
essential fragrances, we choose our own life formula by selecting the values
that we want to include. Rabbi Sager shared with me his writings about some
of his mentors, along with how he'd represent them in his box:

- **"Ronald Braunier,** the core rabbinic teacher at the Recon-
  structionist College during my second year, made it possible
  to ask questions unencumbered by the fear that they were silly.
  His genius was an ability to find the redemptive, meaningful
  core of every question. From him I learned to strive to uphold
  every question. My 'keepsake' would be an index card of the
  sort upon which I would scribble my questions when they

occurred to me at odd hours.

- **Norman Newberg** remains a study in patience and slow process. Theater, poetry, and deep connections of texts and souls are his forte. I consult him regularly and learn from him regularly. My 'keepsake' would be the aroma of the coffee that he would slowly make before every class held in his living room. If the keepsake has to be more tangible, I would make it a copy of Bruno Bettelheim's *The Uses of Enchantment*.

- **Zalman Schachter** taught me much about the soul of a text and how to carefully carry it gently and respectfully across the border into another language. He also taught me by example of prayer's beauty and power. Representing Zalman, I would keep a copy of an early translation that I made for him of a teaching by Rabbi Nahman Brastlav.

- **Art Green**, ironically, taught me the same lessons about prayer. But whereas Zalman taught with a beautiful voice, Art's lessons came through expression (he has no singing voice). I could see in his face that he was speaking to a presence beyond him and within him. His personal encounter with God and with himself taught me to treat both with love and respect. I would keep Art's inscribed copy of his book about Nahman, *Tormented Master*.

- **Judah Goldin** was an elegant master of texts and of language. His love for midrash (textual interpretation) embraced the line between the most academic and the most hospitable to the ancient themes and their teachers. He infused me with a love of midrash that still moves me every time I teach or learn. My deteriorating copy of *Mekhilta de-Rabbi Ismael* is the dearest keepsake that I have of Dr. Goldin.

- **David Hartman** taught me the value of conversation between ancient text and living experience. Here is the only place where 'theology' is personally relevant to most of us. Rabbis must learn this lesson. I was honored to learn from a master. My notebooks of his lectures are my treasures of him."

Reflect and Take Action

- Create a timeline of memorable teachers and mentors and what you learned from each one of them.
- If you're boxing for an elderly person, ask them about the teachers and mentors who had an impact in their life and why. This could be quite a valuable opportunity for a meaningful conversation!

Our Teachers Are Everywhere

I've asked a few friends who their mentors and teachers are. These are a few of their answers:

- the CEO of the company I joined twenty years ago, from whom, every time I was with him, I learned something that I remember and apply many years later
- a neighbor, who taught me about community involvement, whose actions made me aspire to be a better person
- my boss, who truly cared about spending time with me and supporting my development
- a professor, who was passionate about teaching, who always came prepared, who was unselfish with his time, and whose enthusiasm was contagious
- my golf coach in high school, who taught me about life, not just about golf
- the chair of the organization I lead, who has a unique way of discovering a person's interests and passions and finding common ground on which to connect
- my mother, who taught me that it's possible to pursue your own path while being kind and generous to those around you

Finally, I want to share what a friend told me when I asked her which of her mentors she is grateful for. She said, "I want to thank life and time. Life and time are the best teachers. Life teaches us to enjoy time. Time teaches us to enjoy life." There's so much wisdom in those words!

Our Children's Mentors

A few years ago, I gave each of my children their first version of a Box of Life as a Hanukkah gift. In their boxes I included meaningful things I've collected for them over the years. Watching their faces of wonder when they opened their boxes and found what they never knew I'd saved was priceless.

Among the things I kept was an email that John Budwine, my son's high school golf coach and of blessed memory, sent to the team after a bad performance. Coincidentally, out of that team came Doc Redman, now a PGA Tour professional—and he too received this email:

Date: March 7, 2013, 8:55:44 PM EST
Subject: today's play

Our play today was less than stellar. I am very disappointed at the way we played this afternoon at our HOME course.

Even though the other team showed up with less than they needed, today was a day for each of you to show me how you handle a LITTLE pressure. Needless to say, YOU FAILED MISERABLY in proving to me that you guys are ready to play. I am tired of hearing ALL of the excuses. We all can make excuses for our bad play! You guys have got to learn that golf is as much a mental game as it is a physical one. All of you have the physical capabilities to play this game at a high level, but none of you are MENTALLY ready. Too often I see you "GIVING UP" after a bad shot or hole.

Each of you MUST change your attitude toward your golf game and the team. We have a lot of talent that is going wasted because we are not prepared. When I talk about being prepared, I am not talking about hitting a few balls, doing a little chipping, then hitting ten putts. YOU must get your attitude ready to play each shot to the best of your ability!! I have been playing golf for over forty years and I wish I had someone who prepared me mentally for the golf game.

I did not have the good fortune of having a swing coach, custom-fit clubs, or any of the luxuries afforded to each of you.

Your golf swings are very good and solid, but your minds are not coexisting with your games. I will be out of town for the next four days and you do not have any required practices or play days. I want each of you to read the book *Golf Is Not a Game of Perfect* by Dr. Bob Rotella by our next practice on the eighteenth. After you have read this book, I want each of you to write me a couple of paragraphs about how you will MENTALLY prepare for your next round.

If I don't have this from you by the eighteenth, you will not be eligible to participate in ANY matches until you have submitted this to me!!!

"A MIND IS A TERRIBLE THING TO WASTE."

AFTER READING THIS EMAIL, EACH OF YOU MUST SEND ME A RESPONSE **TONIGHT!!!!!**

John Budwine
Director of Instruction
John Budwine Golf Academy
"Callaway Advisory Staff"

I found Budwine's note brilliant. I could see the impact he had on Ilan and his teammates. I liked the fact that Budwine always made sure that his golfers learned more than just how to excel physically on the golf course—he cared about the whole person.

By giving a jumpstart to my children's boxes, I was telling them how much I care about their lives and treasure their experiences. I was also sharing the things I learned through and with them. My hope was that by starting them on the process of boxing at a young age, a process that involves actively thinking about what matters to them, I'd help set them on a path toward a purposeful, thoughtful life.

- If you are boxing for your children, and you know about a teacher who made a positive impact on them, take or find a picture of them and jot down how they were special. If you have correspondence or reports from that teacher, include those too.

> "I never teach my pupils. I only attempt to provide the conditions in which they can learn."
>
> —Albert Einstein

Chapter 11

Traditions and the Aromas and Tastes of Our Soul

"Tradition is a guide and not a jailer."
—W. Somerset Maugham

he word *tradition* is defined in the Merriam-Webster dictionary as "the handing down of information, beliefs, and customs by word of mouth or by examples from one generation to another without written instruction." This makes sense as traditions are beliefs and behaviors with symbolic meaning that are passed down from generation to generation. They tell a story about our identity and connect people from different eras. They can be religious, cultural, familial—or they can be unique to your immediate family. They give us a sense of belonging and stability and tend to create lasting memories.

Those of us who come from a home that celebrates traditions can attest to the powerful bonding they cultivate, connecting us to our family values and roots. Like plant roots, traditions not only ground us, but they also nourish us.

Traditions keep us stable amid change. Moving from country to country as a child, when everything was new and seemed strange, traditions kept me in touch with the familiar. Wherever we went, there was always a Shabbat dinner or a Passover seder, and it felt as if it were tailor-made for us; we always felt at home.

I make a point to keep traditions alive. On every occasion that calls for it, I use my orthodox great-grandfather's kiddush cup; with this tradition, I am acting as the "keeper of the flame." I also use my *savta's* candlesticks to light the Shabbat candles every Friday night. This ritual is an easy way to honor and remember her on a weekly basis. Both objects are in my Box of Life, represented by a photograph and a description of the family tradition I'm memorializing.

My mother-in-law lighting the Shabbat candles with my daughter

I asked my neighbor Mehul about a few of his family traditions. He told me, "Our family is from India, where there is a culture with strong roots in families living together, with many generations under the same roof. This tradition has had a very positive influence in our lives, and we continue having three generations living together in our own house, even here in the United States. In India it's also very common to speak multiple languages—we cherish and treasure our language. We take pride in passing on this heritage to our children and grandchildren. The fact that our eleven-year-old can speak very easily with his grandparents and other family members in Gujarati is a direct advantage of both of these cultures."

During one of our conversations about traditions, Charles quoted American essayist Ralph Waldo Emerson and asked me to write it down (he knew we were both quote freaks). It reads, "Every man is a quotation from all his ancestors." Charles then added that every tradition we keep is part of that quotation and went on to tell me that Mahler asserts that "tradition is not the worship of ashes but the preservation of fire," which to me was a very powerful statement. Give it some thought!

- What rituals and traditions can you recall from your child-hood? Do you know where they came from? Which do you continue to honor to this day?
- What objects are associated with your traditions? How might you commemorate these in your box?
- What five traditions would you like to preserve and pass on? Jot down what these mean to you and include photos, stories, or videos.
- Have any family traditions fallen by the wayside? If you can, interview a family member about these and share their story.

Holiday Traditions

The holidays are times many of us associate with traditions. People hide eggs at Easter, watch fireworks on the Fourth of July, carve pumpkins at Halloween, sing carols at Christmastime, and the list goes on and on.

New Year's Eve is celebrated around the globe and is filled with different traditions. In my household we honor a tradition that started in Spain but has spread from there, especially to Latin America, where people eat twelve grapes starting twelve minutes before midnight. While we do so, we each make twelve wishes, and they all need to be made before the clock strikes midnight. Other New Year's Eve traditions involve wearing white for good luck, eating fish as your main entrée because fish always swim forward, kissing those around you at midnight as an indication that whoever we are with at that moment predicts what type of luck we will have for the rest of the year, eating round foods that will lead to prosperity, and eating black-eyed peas to bring luck and peace for the rest of the year.

Our family has a unique New Year's Eve tradition passed on to us by my mother-in-law. The females in the family wear brand-new pink panties to welcome the year. If you ask me why we do it, my answer is, "I don't know. It is simply a tradition." I love it because it keeps my mother-in-law present—thirteen of her descendants wear pink underwear as we welcome a new journey around the sun. And now you know something very private about me!

Reflect and Take Action

- Think about your holiday traditions. Are there any that are unique to your family? How can you help keep that tradition alive?
- Ask your oldest relatives how they celebrated holidays and which were their most memorable ones. See if you can find holiday photographs from your ancestors. The details you notice will provide you with clues about their traditions.

Childhood Traditions

Many of our holiday traditions are centered around kids—trick or treating at Halloween, egg hunts at Easter, and presents from Santa at Christmas. Perhaps this is because we are more likely to continue traditions that we learn as children. One universal childhood experience is losing our baby teeth, and there are many traditions around this rite of passage. In my case it was El Ratón Pérez, a cute, friendly mouse who grabbed my baby teeth from under my pillow and replaced them with treats or coins. For my kids it was the tooth fairy.

In writing this chapter, I realized that I had no idea where the tooth fairy tradition came from, so I did a little research. I learned that it started as a folktale from the Middle Ages. Legend has it that Europeans believed a witch could curse someone using their teeth, so it was important to dispose of baby teeth. Every tooth was buried, swallowed, left for rodents to eat, or even burned. It was believed that a tooth fed to a rodent would contribute to the development of a healthy adult tooth. The tooth fairy myth began to shape itself as a fairy tale in eighteenth-century France. *La Bonne Petite Souris*, a bedtime story written by Madame d'Aulnoy, tells the tale of a fairy that changes into a mouse to help a queen defeat an evil king. The mouse secretly hides under the evil king's pillow and defeats him by knocking out his teeth.

You might be wondering, Why does the tooth fairy leave money under the pillow? The idea of exchanging a tooth for coins originated in Scandinavia. Vikings paid children for lost teeth. Teeth were worn on necklaces as good-luck charms in battle. The tooth fairy of modern times didn't make an appearance until the 1900s, but tooth myths and rites of passage have existed in many cultures since the dawn of time.

When speaking with me about traditions, my friend Diane shared, "One of my earliest memories is of my mother tucking my brother and me into bed at night and having us recite the Lord's Prayer. It was a nightly ritual for us. When I became a mother, it was one I carried on with my daughter. We often said the Lord's Prayer before bed, and I also taught her to recite it whenever she was scared or anxious to calm herself and feel grounded.

"On a more practical front, my mother insisted that we make our beds every morning before we left for school. We also had to make them properly! While I'm not the most organized person, nor particularly orderly with my things, to this day, I rarely leave my bed unmade. It's an ingrained ritual for me, thanks to my mother." Like Diane, most of us have rituals we grew up with, and many of these have become traditions we pass on to the next generation.

New Traditions

Many traditions are centuries old, but it's certainly possible to make new ones. Every family has their own special way of doing things, and with time and repetition, they can become traditions. Andrea, a fellow coach and friend, shared, "A family tradition we have is decorating the kitchen counter for birthdays, anniversaries, first days of school, holidays, and lots of other excuses to celebrate. I wake up early, quietly set up the display, and patiently wait for the boys to wake up. Once all are awake, Chris and I make breakfast, and we all listen to music and spend time enjoying our treats together." Andrea started a tradition for her family, but she might be surprised when her sons become adults and continue this beautiful tradition they shared growing up.

Another friend told me that she started taking nighttime walks with her kids when the moon is full. They marvel at how much light the moon gives and how much they can see, yet how different it looks during the day.

Commemorating moments like these in our Box of Life is invaluable for those who one day might ask, "Where does this family tradition come from?" If you start a new tradition, record it along with the thinking behind it so generations to come can learn about its origins.

Reflect and Take Action

- Does your family have any traditions that are unique? What are they and how did they begin?
- Are there any traditions you've admired and would like to start incorporating into your life now? What about them appeals to you? How can you make it happen?
- If you're boxing for someone else, ask them about the traditions they observed.

All Types of Traditions

I've enjoyed asking random people about traditions they keep and who those traditions started with. Following are some of their responses:

- We set up sleeping bags and sleep in front of the Christmas tree with the kids as I always did with my cousins at our family's mountain cabin.
- We send a favorite book with any birthday gift, as my mom always did.
- We all wear red when a family member has a birthday, no matter where we live. It was started by my great-grandmother and is still going in our family.
- We add an extra candle for every birthday, which represents a wish for another year to come, as my mother said we should always do.
- Being Jewish, my family and I eat Chinese food and go to the movies on Christmas Eve when Christians are all celebrating with their families.
- We have a secret family handshake.

Tastes of Times Past

Traditions and food are interlinked. Family gatherings often revolve around eating together, and most of us associate certain foods with specific holidays—Irish soda bread on St. Patrick's Day, hot cross buns at Easter, latkes for Hannukah, gingerbread men at Christmas, pumpkin pie at Thanksgiving . . . The familiarity of these meals makes them all the more meaningful to us. In his book *Eating Animals*, Jonathan Safran Foer writes, "Stories about food are stories about us—our history and our values. Within my family's Jewish tradition, I came to learn that food serves two parallel purposes: it nourishes, and it helps you remember. Eating and storytelling are inseparable—the saltwater is also tears; the honey not only tastes sweet, but makes us think of sweetness; the matzo is the bread of our affliction."[1]

Journalist Orge Castellano's story in *The Nosher*, titled "Food tells our story, roots!" supports Foer's theory that our traditions around food form an intrinsic part of who we are. Castellano shared that family recipes helped him discover his hidden family history, writing, "I only found that I was Jewish as a teenager, and that all our colorful, fragrant, crunchy dishes were deeply rooted in Judaic culinary traditions from sixteenth-century Spain. That the ingredients and aromas of my mom's kitchen resembled dishes from the Sephardic gastronomy repertoire."[2] His family was expelled from Spain. They arrived in South America, where they discreetly practiced Jewish rituals, living in fear of the inquisition. He writes, "Reconnecting with my roots through foods during these difficult times has helped me to cope with stress, anxiety, and loneliness . . . I'll continue paying homage to each and every one of the dishes that my family preserved with such dedication and courage. This is the only way I can celebrate—and always carry with me—their everlasting legacy."

My cousin Clarita also keeps the memory of departed family members

---

[1]   "A Trip Down Memory Lane." *The Gluttons Digest*, 23 May 2011, www.thegluttons-digest.com/a-trip-down-memory-lane/.

[2]   Castellano, Orge. "Cooking Helped Me Discover My Family's Hidden Jewish History." *The Nosher*, 7 Jan. 2021, www.myjewishlearning.com/the-nosher/cooking-helped-me-discover-my-familys-hidden-jewish-history/.

alive through food. She shared with me that "one of the most important people in my life was my mother-in-law, Rosita. She taught me her recipes for Passover. She died many years ago, but every Passover I feel I'm with her again in the kitchen. I inherited her handwritten recipe book, which is better to me than any jewelry or crown I could have received."

She went on to talk about how food links the generations: "My grandmother prepared essigfleisch, a sour-sweet meat stew that was delicious. My dad learned to cook it before the illness that took him away from us. When I think about both of them together, I can taste the essigfleisch. I'm now the one making it and teaching my adult kids to prepare it as well."

Clarita continued, "My mom taught me how to bake a corn cake with béchamel. It became one of my kids' favorite dishes. My son learned how to prepare it and now I'm teaching his girlfriend. All of those who left us taught me how to provide love and pampering through their dishes. And it is always a source of joy when I see my kids keeping those traditions."

My friend and colleague Eric shared with pride, "My wife still makes fudge in the way she learned from my mother, and my mother learned it from her mother, my grandmother." I can only imagine the chocolatey fragrance in Eric's home and all the people who come back to his life with every savory bite of it.

> *"Cooking is all about people. Food is maybe the only universal thing that really has the power to bring everyone together. No matter what culture, everywhere around the world, people eat together."*
> —Guy Fieri

Charles's Kitchen

"Breaking bread," or sharing a meal, was Charles's way of fostering a new connection and establishing a friendship. I heard him use that expression often. To invite you to break bread meant to invite you into a companionship. He believed that eating together was the best way to express to someone a genuine intention to become their friend.

Charles always said that every challenge or misunderstanding among people, when approached around a table sharing a meal, would be solved and even strengthen the relationship. "Food brings people together, Orit. Never forget it," he told me.

Charles enjoyed cooking and experimenting in the kitchen. Cooking was a way for him to be creative, a form of art. He told me that his mother taught him how to cook, and he became so good at cooking that he was able to go by feel. In his box I found a few recipes, such as the following for potato pancakes:

Charles M. Stern whipping up some whole-wheat pancakes

Potato Pancake Recipe from Charles's Box

Ingredients:

5 large potatoes, shredded

1 large onion, grated

3 eggs

1/3 cup matzo meal

1 tsp. salt

¼ tsp. black pepper

1/3 cup vegetable oil, for frying

Squeeze water out of potatoes and add grated onion. Mix well. Beat the eggs well and add matzo meal, salt, and pepper. Add the egg mixture to the potatoes. Mix well. Heat oil in a frying pan. Form 4" patties, not more than 1/3 inch thick, and brown on both sides. Place on paper towels and put into the oven to keep warm until serving.

Reflect and Take Action

- Which five dishes do you cherish or are known for and want to pass on? Include recipes, photos, stories, or videos of you preparing them.
- Do you have recipes that have been handed down through your family? Gather them together and make sure to include information about where they came from and whether they are prepared for any special occasion.
- What is your favorite comfort food? Why? Tell the story behind it.
- List your three favorite restaurants. Share their location and why they're your favorites.
- If you're boxing for someone else, include their favorite foods. If you're boxing for your kids, consider a favorite foods time-line. It's amazing how they change—and also stay the same!

A Meaningful (and Tasty) Gift

I wasn't sure what to get my dad for his eightieth birthday. He was blessed to have everything he needed and was at a stage in which more *stuff* was meaningless. Still, I knew I wanted to give him a meaningful experience, and the solution I came to was creating a basket with foods from Argentina and Israel. I ordered all his favorites, including cookies, olive oil, a variety of teas, pasta, candy, chocolate, cereals, etc. My goal was to take him on a journey through flavor to his favorite places, people, and memories. I also translated this chapter of my book into Spanish and attached it to the basket, as I wasn't sure if he would be alive when the book was published. My gift was a success!

Sniffing the World

A neuroscientist friend told me that our sense of smell is more closely linked with our memory than any other of our senses, with taste as a close second. Recent studies show that the part of the brain (the retrosplenial cortex) that stores and recalls memories may be the same part that integrates experienced sensations (touch, smell, and taste, for example). The retrosplenial cortex is associated with our episodic memory, the type of memory that records events in our minds. Because of this association, memories are often sparked by a smell or sensation.

A smell's ability to trigger memories is known as "the Proust effect," after the French writer Marcel Proust. In his novel *À la recherche du temps perdu (In Search of Lost Time),* he famously described how the experience of eating a madeleine transported him back to his childhood. He wrote in detail how it triggered memories about his aunt's "old gray house upon the street . . . and with the house the town, from morning to night and in all weathers, the square where I used to be sent before lunch, the street along which I used to run errands, the country roads we took when it was fine." In short, one bite of a small cake brought his past flooding back in vivid detail!

There are aromas and tastes that we never forget and are an important part of our story. One day we might be able to reproduce and save smells as we do with visual images via photographs and digital media. But until that day arrives, we can only describe the aromas of our lives using our best writing skills to make sure they are included in our Box of Life. In my box, I'll do my best to re-create the aromas of my mother-in-law's and *savta's* kitchens. Every time I walked into those kitchens, I was embraced in love. Of course, I'll also include their recipes in my Box of Life. Another emblematic smell I want to capture is that of fresh-baked cookies, as it reminds me of Charles; that was the aroma he always welcomed me with when I visited him.

My daughter shared that the smell of fresh *asado* takes her back to "el country," where we would weekend away from the city when we lived in Argentina. And the smell of mothballs transports her to her great-grandmother's house.

I've asked a number of people to share what smells evoke special memories for them, and they provided a bouquet of fragrances:

- The smell of chocolate reminds me of my grandmother. She would always have the best chocolate in her kitchen drawer. In my box I have the last chocolate wrapper I ever opened in her house before she passed.

- The smell of sunscreen reminds me of the fun days at the beach with my cousins when my aunt was obsessed with covering us all until we couldn't be any whiter. I have a picture of my aunt chasing us with the sunscreen firmly in her hand.

- The smell of fresh-cut grass reminds me of my dad mowing the lawn and "hiring" me as his little helper. I have a picture I painted in third grade of me with my dad hard at work.

- Puppy breath reminds me of all my puppy love. I have created a photo collage of all of the puppies I've had in my life—ten of them in total.

- The smell of pine trees reminds me of my naps with my mom in the forest in our backyard. I have a beautiful photograph captured by my dad.

- The smell of wood burning transports me to the campfires I made with my friends. I have a CD with all the songs we sang around the flickering flames.

- The smell of any city reminds me of Buenos Aires, where I was born and lived for thirty-five years. I have a postcard of industrial Buenos Aires next to one of New York and one of Paris.

Reflect and Take Action

- What are your favorite smells? Why? Jot down a few thoughts and recollections about these.
- Are there any aromas that trigger memories of a specific event or time in your life? Are they something you'd like to capture in your box?
- Is there a smell that you associate with your home? If yes, what is it? Something cooking on the stove? Incense burning? Perfume? Your dog?

"Ways to my heart:
1. Buy me food.
2. Make me food.
3. Be food."
—Unknown

Chapter 12

The Places That Matter

"Favorite people, favorite places, favorite memories of the past. These are the joys of a lifetime. Those are the things that last."

—Henry van Dyke

Have you noticed that when we tell a story, we often start by sharing where it took place? (Once upon a time, in a far-off wood . . .) Or that when recalling an impactful event, we tend to ask, "Where were you when you heard about (insert event)?" There's no doubt that place has a profound impact on our experiences and in shaping who we are.

We all have places in our lives that are special to us. They may be very familiar, such as our home, they may be places we visit only occasionally, or they may even be spots we've been just once. But for whatever reason, we have a strong attachment to that place. Perhaps something special happened there—you did or felt something for the first time. Or perhaps the place is so well known to you that it feels like part of your DNA.

We can capture these places in our box in a variety of ways. The first step is to identify them. Think back on the places you've visited and what they've meant to you. This may be a powerful journey. When we revisit places that made an impact on our lives, even if that revisiting is only through viewing old photos or reading letters or articles, a number of different things can happen:

- **We retrieve long-forgotten memories that have been out of mind for a considerable time.** When Charles looked at a picture of an art gallery in San Antonio where he participated in an exhibit, he immediately shared stories about the people he met on opening night. When I look at pictures of my homes throughout my life, I immediately recall adventures we had while living there.

- **We recover faded episodes and reacquaint them with our self-defining, autobiographical memories, which can become very satisfying.** Our memory can remind us of lessons drawn from certain experiences. Charles's art gallery photo reminded him that he only exhibited there because he had the courage ("chutzpah," as he called it) to stop by and show them his art. "Chutzpah can open many doors, Orit," he said while looking at the gallery picture.

- **We correct altered memories.** Sometimes the memory of a place can help us refresh our recollection of what really happened there. Charles was at first confused about when he first exhibited his miniature statues, but as soon as he saw the picture of the art gallery, he remembered.

Memorable Places

Have you ever wondered why we remember certain places more than others? When we enter a room, for example, our brains record the location of objects, such as pieces of furniture, bookshelves, and windows. We most likely will not remember the arrangement of that place unless something memorable happened there. Perhaps that's why Charles's home office is memorable to me. I clearly remember his majestic desk, the many books on the bookshelves to the right of his desk chair, and the many small objects and papers sitting on his desk. It is, after all, a place where I listened to life stories and the place where I was trusted to embark on what turned out to be the Box of Life Project and this book.

Special Places

When asking people what their special places are, I heard a variety of answers:

- the summer camp where I met my best friends
- the state fair I would go to every year with my family and friends
- the ice cream parlor next to my parents' house, where my dad would take me whenever I got an acceptable report card
- the train station where I met my husband
- my college dorm in which many firsts happened
- the beach house I used to go to with my family for my dad's birthday
- the bridge where I used to go as a teenager whenever I wanted some alone time
- the drive-in movie theater where I had my first kiss
- the Thanksgiving table at my mom's house
- the coffee shop where I wrote my thesis
- the Hospital Cancer Center where I learned that I won the battle

As you can see, this is a diverse collection of places, but they share some commonalities. Many of them are places we shared with people we care about. A friend once told me, "I don't have a favorite place. I have my favorite people. And, whenever I'm with my favorite people, it becomes my favorite place." His efforts to build community wherever he was and in all stages of his life are reflected in his box. It was the people who made places special for him.

Another thing that makes a place special is a memorable or meaningful experience that happened there, such as a cancer-free diagnosis or a first kiss. And then there are the places that make us feel in certain ways. Margot, my wonderful book-editing coach and friend, shared with me that her special place is "the summer cottage where my family has gone for three generations. Run down and beautiful, it's a place where I can truly relax and set aside the demands of working life. The sounds are those of nature—wind, insects, birds—and the views are of sky, water, and trees. A slice of heaven." I suggested that Margot include in her box a few photos of the cottage, the address, a story or more of what happened in that cottage, and why it became her special place.

Sometimes a special place is one that it is hard to go back to because it's associated with heartbreaking memories. To me, those places are worth remembering as well. For good or for bad, they had an impact on our lives. It was hard for me to go back to the restaurant where I had lunch with my husband on March 17, 1992, the day the Israeli Embassy was bombed in Buenos Aires. We were close enough to the bombing to feel the restaurant shake, as if it would fall. I remember being confused about what was happening and dashing into the street, where dozens of people pushed past me, running in panic, many with blood on their faces. I remember the despair I felt when I realized what was going on. That restaurant that I used to love is a place I don't want to go back to, and yet is a place I won't forget. When I talk about what happened that day, I always start by sharing where I was.

Reflect and Take Action

- Of all the places you have been to, where would you choose to be transported right now? Why? Commemorate those places in your box. You might use captioned photos, postcards, brochures, maps, mementos, or souvenirs.
- To determine which places should inhabit your Box of Life, set aside time for a trip down memory lane and recall specific places from your past. Let your mind wander back to different periods of time.
- Create a timetable of places that became important to you at different points in your life.
- If you're boxing for someone else, be sure to include their special places.
- When boxing for children, include things that will help them remember details from their childhood that usually fade. For example, you could include photos of your first home, their room, their favorite places growing up, a map of the town they were born in, and the different places they lived if they moved.

Home

Dorothy from *The Wizard of Oz* reminded us, "There's no place like home," and for many of us this truly is the case. Home is a place where we can relax, feel comfortable, and truly be ourselves. Based on what Charles told me and what I found in his box, I can say that for him, home was San Antonio, TX, even though he got there later in life. "The people and the community I immersed myself in made it home," he wrote in an article I found in his box. Every time he mentioned San Antonio, I could see a spark in his eye.

For me, home is complex. Even after living in the United States for twenty-five years, the longest I've ever been in one country, I still feel like the new kid on the block. I still don't understand many of the local jokes, parenting styles, traditions, cultural trends, and history as well as I would like to. Whenever I say "hello" to someone new, the follow-up question I get is, "Where are you from?" My response is a lot to take in: "I was born in Israel to Argentinean parents and grew up in many countries, including Costa Rica, El Salvador, Ecuador, Argentina, and Colombia." And although I feel at home in my house, whenever I travel back to Israel or Argentina, I hear myself saying, "I'm going home." Then, when I'm there, despite their deep familiarity, I sometimes feel like a stranger in both countries. And when I fly back to North Carolina, I'm traveling home again.

So in a way, many places are home to me, and every single country I lived in is part of my box. They are present through photographs, postcards, letters, recipes, old address books, and of course through stories.

Thinking about the meaning of "home" prompted me to ask others, "Where is home for you?" Again I received a variety of answers:

- where I can be myself and be loved for it
- where my friends and family are
- church
- where my bed is
- my hometown
- at my parents' house
- wherever I pay my taxes
- any place where I feel safe
- wherever I am living

For American memoirist, teacher, and journalist Mark Matousek, "home is where we find our balance, the pivoting point that connects us to the earth."[1] Someone once told me that home is where you want to be buried or have your ashes scattered. In a TED Talk, essayist and novelist Pico Iyer

---

[1]   Mark Matousek, "Where Is Home," *Huff Post*, January 7, 2017, www.huffpost.com/entry/where-is-home_b_8926636.

stated, "For more and more of us, home has less to do with a piece of soil than a piece of soul."[1]

He estimates that more than 220 million people are not living in their country of origin. He is 100 percent Indian by blood and ancestry, but he was born and grew up in England and lived in the United States and Japan. Based on his personal experiences, he concluded, "Home is not only the place where you sleep, but it's the place where you stand." I recommend watching his TED Talk titled "Where Is Home?"

I moved between countries before I had the opportunity to fully develop my own cultural identity, consequently becoming a cultural chameleon. Charles thought that was what made me "empathetic" and "a good active listener." He said, "You had to learn how to understand others so you could speak the same cultural language they did." This belief was reassuring to me in times of self-doubt. The reality for me is, like the Argentinean singer and songwriter Facundo Cabral wisely wrote, "No soy de aquí, ni soy de allá . . ." (I'm not from here, nor am I from there . . .).

At the end of the day, I believe my mother had it right. Where we were as a family was home. Every time we were in a new country, she made sure it felt like home: a safe place in which I could be who I was, where my belongings were always safe, and where I had the familiar comfort I needed. The rituals observed in my house were always the same, including dinners as a family and lighting the Shabbat candles every Friday evening. In my box, I have pictures of each one of my homes that include the address in case the next generations in my family decide to take a trip back in time and follow their ancestors' footsteps.

> *"We shape our homes, and then our homes shape us."*
> —Winston Churchill

---

[1] Pico Iyer, "Where Is Home," *TED*, March 11, 2014, www.ted.com/talks/pico_iyer_where_is_home.

- Where is home for you? Is it your childhood or current home, or perhaps both, or neither? What makes it "home"? How does it feel compared to other places?
- What five things about your home do you want to include in your box? What are some ways you could represent it?
- If you're boxing for someone else, ask them about their homes. What made them special?

Happy Places

We often hear people refer to their *happy place*. For many this is an actual place that brings pleasure of one kind or another. My friend Isabel loves being in her garden—watching things change and grow is both calming and energizing for her. Tim, a coaching client, loves spending time in his woodworking shop. He gets deep pleasure discovering the different aspects of the wood and gets lost in his projects, losing all sense of time. My son Ilan's happy place is on the golf course, where he enjoys nature and the company of his fellow golfers.

Charles's happy place was wherever he was when working with the community, engaged in learning, flowing in creativity, being someone of relevance, or solving a challenge. To him, it was more about the experience than the place itself. In Charles's box I found articles in which he was at his happy place—articles in which he described taking a trip or spending time in a community, an art studio or gallery, a theater stage, a radio station, or at his desk writing an article or a play script.

Don, in his early sixties, included in his box a picture of a bench next to a soccer field. Attached to the picture, the text reads, "This is one of my happy places. It was my high school hot spot, where we hung out after school and during the weekends. This is where many of my best high school memories happened and where I felt cool and loved. It is at that bench that I met my sweetheart and I developed lasting friendships."

Priscilla, who is creating her Box of Life, included in her box a small tile, about which she wrote, "This tile is from my mom's kitchen, one of my happy places. It's where I spent time with my mom—chatting, crying, arguing, laughing, and enjoying many other treasured moments together. It was a cozy space and had everything I loved, which my mom would make sure was there for me."

Heading the list of my happy places is my home, especially when it's full of family. After that comes the ocean. Being with family and friends at the ocean is heaven! And just like Charles, there are experiences that make a place a happy one for me. Usually, it is when I'm engaged in a project in which I can feel relaxed and surrounded by positive energy, flow, and the notion that I'm making a difference and growing personally and professionally.

Reflect and Take Action

- What are your happy places? What makes these places so pleasurable?
- How can you capture those places in your Box of Life?

Musical Journeys

You might be wondering why music appears in a chapter about places. And yet think about how hearing a song can transport us to places and times gone by. Music is a powerful trigger of nostalgia and evokes memories and the emotions associated with them. No matter who you are, certain chords and lyrics have the power of taking you back in time.

I was sitting next to my dad in his home-hospice hospital bed on a day when he seemed confused, anxious, and hopeless. Not sure how to make him feel better, I grabbed his dusty old CD player and began to play Hebrew melodies that he used to enjoy. My daughter and I burst into tears when, with a smile on his face, he suddenly started singing "Yaase Shalom," a classic Israeli song based on a prayer for peace, titled "He Who Makes Peace." I could clearly see in his body language that the melody transported him to a different place and time, one where he felt young and filled with ideals, dreams, and hopes. I can't argue with a quote I once read: "Each memory has a soundtrack of its own."

There are many studies on the effect music has on our brains and memories. University of Melbourne neuropsychologist Amee Baird's research focuses on relationships and how people and their partners navigate life together after a brain injury or disease. She found that couples who listened together to a "special song" that was significant to their relationship felt that this reminiscing strengthened their bond—and possibly even alleviated the effects of dementia.[1]

Dalia, my sister-in-law, told me, "Sometimes, when I'm alone in the car driving, I enjoy songs that take me back to different moments of the past. And those are "my moments." A song that still makes me dance, one that still makes me feel something special throughout my body and soul, a song that used to make me cry and now makes me smile . . . one that reminds me of a certain love from my past." Music is like a time machine that can vividly conjure memories that otherwise might have been lost.

In my box, I have a list of songs that mean something to me, including their lyrics and why they are special. Do you have songs or music genres that make you nostalgic? Listen to them and feel where they take you. Often there are stories, messages, or memories attached to these songs that may be worth including in your box. Imagine your great-grandchild listening to that *same music*, knowing what it meant to you. Powerful!

---

[1]   A. Baird and S. Samson, "Music evoked autobiographical memory after severe acquired brain injury: Preliminary findings from a case series." *Neuropsychological rehabilitation*, November 21, 2013, 10.1080/09602011.2013.858642.

- What three songs or melodies evoke a special emotion every time you listen to them? What memories do they evoke? Share the story behind them.
- Create a timeline of your favorite singers or bands throughout your lifetime.
- What music do you remember your parents and grandparents listening to while you were growing up? What music did they like to dance to? How do you feel when you hear these tunes?

———

The places we choose to preserve in our boxes are special. They are either places that mean a lot to us, places we want others to know about, or places we don't want to forget about, even when our memory fails us. The places we cherish are part of our story, and their presence in our Box of Life is essential to understanding our cultural background and journey on earth.

> *"When you leave a beautiful place, you carry it with you wherever you go."*
> —Alexandra Stoddard

Chapter 13

Heirlooms, Talismans, Mementos, and Objects

"Between what a man calls me and what he simply calls mine, the line is difficult to draw."

—**William James**

W e all have things that are precious to us because of the feelings they evoke. Objects hold powerful associations, reminding us of people and places we hold dear, important events in our lives, and eras we lived through.

American philosopher, historian, and psychologist William James believed that our possessions define who we are—that apart from being useful, they represent our extended selves. Author Tim O'Brien expressed a similar idea in his novel, *The Things They Carried*. Through stories about a platoon of American soldiers fighting during the Vietnam War, O'Brien distills the essence of each soldier by listing things they carried with them. For example, Lieutenant Jimmy Cross carries letters from his true love, Martha, in his backpack and her good-luck pebble in his mouth. Other soldiers carry marijuana, a girl-friend's pantyhose, a pocketknife, and the New Testament. O'Brien likens the soldiers' physical objects to the emotional burdens that they bear.

Think about it and look around you. If you are the sum of your possessions, who are you?

Ingrid Fetell Lee, author of *Joyful: The Surprising Power of Ordinary Things to Create Extraordinary Happiness*, argues that there is a clear link between our surroundings, including the objects in them, and our well-being. In general, she posits, objects with round, symmetrical shapes elicit positive emotions, while sharp, angular, and asymmetrical forms may contribute to tension and sadness. The author also explains that certain objects resonate positively with us due to our personal attachments to them or their connection to a specific memory. Objects can conjure pleasant feelings, whether they are linked to the past, present, or future. Fetell Lee states, "One of the amazing things about the human brain is that we can feel joy across multiple timescales. We can feel it in the present, of course, but we can also call it back up from the past, and we can anticipate it in the future as you do when you have tickets for an upcoming concert pinned above your desk or a new bathing suit purchased in advance of a trip."[1]

Only those possessions with the power to tell stories and evoke emotions belong in our boxes.

Reflect and Take Action

- Do you carry things with you beyond the usual keys, wallet, phone, etc.? What are they and why do you keep them with you?
- Which twenty objects tell the story of your life? Could you create a timeline with them and attach photographs?

---

[1] Hogan, Brianne. "Why Certain Objects Make Us Happy." *She Knows*, 15 Nov. 2018, www.sheknows.com/health-and'wellnes/articles/1142070/why-objects-make-us-happy/.

Charles's Possessions

While Charles's box contained mostly documents and photos, I was struck by what it conveyed about the things he treasured and his exquisite and sophisticated taste. His box documented his love for books, music, and art.

In it I found photos and articles about his art. Through newspaper clippings I discovered the music he appreciated. I learned about the books that had an impact on him from some pages on which he had handwritten summaries and quotes.

During our conversations, he shared the importance of fashion, style, and design. In his box, he included articles he wrote on the topics.

I wish I had asked Charles for one of his beautiful stone rings or, even better, for one of his sculptures. I want them not because of their material value, but because of their sentimental value.

Our Objects' Stories

Nadav had saved a coat-check ticket that had been pinned on his wife's coat on their very first date, which held a lot of significance to him (detailed in chapter 3). But for anyone who wasn't aware of the story behind that coat-check ticket, it would be a meaningless piece of paper. The same goes for all of the objects in our boxes. It's the stories behind them that matter more than the objects themselves.

Kristin told me that she has an artificial rosebud in her box. If you weren't aware that this was among the roses that were sewn into her wedding veil, it would be nothing more than a fake flower. But knowing that roses are her favorite flower, that the rosebud was an aspect of her very special day, and that her mother made her veil adds another dimension to the object.

Joanne, who is putting her box together, shared that she is including "a sample box of many spools of thread that I played with as a child. It symbolizes my love of design and the power of color." Joanne's choice inspired me to include in my box a palette of colors and a brush, along with a few words about my love for painting.

Hearing people's stories and learning about the objects they treasure has given me new insights into them. I realized that I thought I knew these people, but I suddenly understood that there was much more to what I thought I knew, which was deeply gratifying.

Miriam, a good friend, shared with me that she has been keeping in her attic the Star of David that her mom wore during the Holocaust. She didn't know what else to do with such a sad memory, but now she is putting together a Box of Life in honor of her mom, which includes what she knows about her mother's life during the Nazi regime. The star in the box tells a story of perseverance and survival. Although that story overshadows the box, as it did her mother's life, Miriam's mom accomplished many other things through her lifetime that will also be part of her box.

American author Dawn Raffel wrote a short, delightful book called *The Secret Life of Objects*, a memoir presented through a series of short essays that remind us of the stories and memories that objects carry with them. She starts with "The Mug," in which she tells us about a blue mug she took from her mother's house after her sudden death. The mug is decorated with an image of a Picasso bird from the Milwaukee Art Museum, where her mom had served as a docent. Raffel drinks from the mug every morning. She writes that it is "a clay-based receptacle for stimulant, for memory, for story, for tonic for aloneness." It also serves her as a maternal connection: "My mother was visual. I am not. It took me years to notice that next to that triumphant, fractured blue bird, Picasso painted a smaller bird, close enough to feel the large's heat." *The Secret Life of Objects* reminds us of how objects can elicit treasured memories. Raffel's book had a big impact on me, and now I pay more attention to the stories that objects carry within them.

- Walk around your home and pay attention to the stories told by some of the objects you own. Take a photo of the objects that mean the most to you and jot down the stories behind them.
- Ask people you know what objects they would like to preserve. You will learn many anecdotes and facts about their lives that otherwise might never come up.
- If you had to evacuate and take five objects of emotional value with you, which ones would those be? Why?

Objects That Connect Us to Our Heritage

Most families have sentimental objects passed from one generation to another. In such family heirlooms, we uncover archaeological layers of our history. My parents and I visited not only archaeological sites but also many museums as I grew up. Although I would always protest, "This is boring," my dad made me appreciate how museums protect our cultural heritage. I can't remember most of what I saw in each museum in detail, but there's one image that I can't forget—the shoes of those who perished in the Holocaust, which are preserved in the United States Holocaust Memorial Museum in Washington, DC. They are simple, mundane shoes—nothing fancy, the kind we'd likely not assign any sentimental value to. But those shoes tell a horrifying story that should be preserved. Each one of those shoes belonged to a human being, and those human beings walked through hell in them. Since then, shoes have a new meaning to me. Every morning when I put on my shoes, I ask them, "Where are we going today?" Fortunately for most of us, our heirlooms are not as emotionally freighted as those shoes. They serve to connect us to our ancestors and times gone by, reminding us that we are part of a story that began before we were born, a story that is greater than our own. Objects are more than just things—they carry meaning, history, and deep emotional connections.

Diane, a writer, was born in 1965 in Camagüey, Cuba, and immigrated to the United States with her family when she was just thirteen months old. She shared with me, "As Cuban emigrants, my parents (along with my brother and me) were only allowed to take one suitcase per adult. We were not permitted to take any official documents out of the country other than passports, and we weren't allowed any sentimental objects. Thus, I grew up without a birth certificate; my parents didn't have theirs either, nor their marriage certificate. My mother snuck out a few small pictures of her family that, if I recall, she sewed into the lining of clothes in the suitcase. Being caught with those items risked losing permission to immigrate to the United States. I have these photos now and I treasure them. Having so few sentimental objects or documents from my birth land means I probably value these kinds of items more than most people. I've always considered them a critical connection to previous generations and our cultural roots."

I own a samovar (a metal container traditionally used to heat water) from

my mother's side of the family. It's been passed down from generation to generation, but its origins are a mystery. I don't know exactly who used it or where they used it. If it could speak, I imagine it would tell an abundance of stories. As we build our boxes, we need to understand that passing possessions from one generation to the next one is not enough—we also need to pass down the story of those possessions, ideally in a way that will allow others to know us and our ancestors.

I have other family heirlooms that I

I wish my samovar could speak!

treasure. They tell me where I came from and what I value, and they provide me with a sense of purpose, continuity, and comfort. That's the case for the robe I've inherited from my mother-in-law, which embraces me with her warmth and love. A vase that belonged to my paternal grandmother reminds me of the stories I've heard about her; she was a woman of ideals and perseverance. My dad told me that the vase was always filled with red roses, her favorite flowers. My great-great grandfather's kiddush cup—used to bless the wine or grape juice to sanctify the Shabbat and Jewish holidays—transports me in time every Friday night. Holding that cup, I reconnect with all the stories of perseverance it represents: pogroms in the Russian Empire, the Holocaust, two World Wars, major pandemics, and the harsh challenges every generation before us had to face. And yet, that same kiddush cup is still here on our family's table in active use for my generation and the next.

Nathalie told me, "In my Box of Life, I'm including a photograph of an antique ornamental bowl on a pedestal centerpiece that I inherited from my mother and want to pass down to future generations in our family. I'm aware that the antique itself might be lost without a story attached to it. By including this story, I think my descendants will pay more attention to the piece."

The story attached to the heirloom's photograph reads: "My mother loved antiques and instilled that love in me and my sister. She told my father that she would rather have beautiful antiques than jewelry. My father had a service station in downtown Atlanta, and directly behind it was an old Atlanta home owned by Joe Barnes, an antiques dealer. Joe was able to locate many beautiful pieces in the post-war years, and my mom was a ready and willing recipient of some of those treasures. At one point, she purchased this lovely glass epergne that rests in a brass holder as a centerpiece for her dining room table, and it became one of my favorite

Nathalie's photograph of the antique that belonged to her mother

pieces. After her passing, the epergne came to me, and I had it on my dining room table for many years. When I moved, I could not accommodate that table, so the piece went to my daughter Beth. It now adorns her dining room table. I hope that someday it will sit on her daughter's table and that my granddaughter will remember her great-grandmother, as well as her grandmother who adored her. By having the story of this centerpiece in my Box of Life, I hope that it will remain in our family forever."

Reflect and Take Action

- Share a story about five family keepsakes you inherited. How did you acquire these keepsakes? Who gave them to you and when? What are the memories attached to these keepsakes? If you can, include the item or photograph of the item in your box.

Objects That Remind Us of People

Certain objects resonate not only because of their ability to recall memories but because of the person with whom they are associated. That's why we so often get rid of gifts from our exes after a breakup. In contrast, it is hard to let go of gifts that we received from someone we loved who is no longer with us.

During my childhood, my *savta* would mail me letters from Israel to whatever country I was living in. She'd always include stickers in these letters. Over forty years later, I've framed all of them, and they are hanging in my office above my desk. They remind me of my childhood and of my *savta's* love. She taught me that geographic distance is not an impediment to being present and pampering someone you cherish. I also have in my office a framed photo of her carrying me; she's gazing at me in the sweet loving way she always looked at me. That photo makes me feel she is still protecting me today, which I believe she is. She and I played a lot of games together, and every time I see dominos or checkers, I feel her presence. In my box I have a picture of her playing checkers with me, along with a list of all the games we played together and what those games meant to me.

On my nightstand I have a ceramic angel that was given to me by my school friends when I moved from Colombia to Argentina. I was thirteen years old, and that angel has been with me ever since. It reminds me of lasting friendships, people who remain with us even if we don't see them often, and

My savta playing checkers with me

that things can remain the same even through transitions.

My daughter, Maia, always wanted to have something that belonged to her grandma, Babu of blessed memory. During our last trip to Argentina, I gave her an old apron Babu used to wear. Maia hugged the apron and said, "It smells like Babu's kitchen." I could see she was immersed in the memories and feelings the apron conjured. I'm uncertain whether she will ever actually use that apron. Knowing her, she won't so she never has to wash the smells away, but merely having the apron still fulfills the mission of bringing Babu closer to her.

My friend Eric said, "I keep things that my loved ones made with their own hands. Things like furniture made by my grandfather, knickknacks made by my other grandfather, photos from my father, and Christmas decorations made by my grandmother and mother." Now I have a better understanding of why Eric's home becomes a fairy tale during Christmas. He and his family throw one of the best holiday parties in town. It's not just the guests who attend the party; it is also his ancestors who are present.

I've asked a group of people to share what their sentimental possessions are and was not surprised to see how many were connected to loved ones.

Below are a few of their answers:

- I have a memento from my honeymoon in Venice that reminds me of a very romantic trip with my husband of thirty years.
- Now I wear my grandpa's cozy Christmas sweater that he used to wear every year.
- I have my dad's stamp collection that he started in 1956. He used to sit me on his lap whenever he worked on it. I keep it on my desk.
- I wear my dad's watch every day. I'm twenty-nine, and his watch is a reminder to use my time wisely. It's also a way to keep my dad, who died five years ago, close to me.
- I still have the friendship bracelet my best friend gave me when we were in high school over twenty years ago.
- I hang on to the red necklace my grandma gave me for good luck when I was seven, twenty-three years ago! I wear it every time I'm being challenged or feel anxious.
- The Buddha figure that belonged to my aunt protects me. I have it on my nightstand, and I kiss it every morning.

Having mementos close to us after the death of a loved one can be a powerful way to help us grieve. My friend Jenny surprised me with a gift she prepared when my dad went into hospice and gave it to me an hour after he passed. Jenny secretly asked my kids for a T-shirt that my dad wore a lot, and she used it to create a bear. That's right, a bear! She added Israeli and Argentinean flags, along with a message from my dad saying that every time I hug that bear, he is with me. I can't put into words the comfort that this stuffed bear brings me. It is truly the most meaningful gift I have ever received in my life.

Me with Jenny's bear, the day my dad passed

Boxing for a Deceased Loved One

A Box of Life is an excellent way to preserve the memories of a loved one who has passed away. The goal is to do so in a way that honors their life and the mark they left on the world. Their Box of Life can include items that were important to them, such as correspondence, photos, and other memorabilia. Consider including the following:

- videos of the person you are remembering
- letters, cards, and notes you have received from them or written to them
- mementos that commemorate their work, their favorite activities, beloved pets, and more
- souvenirs from special occasions that you shared together, such as milestone celebrations or photos from a vacation
- anything else that reminds you of the person and shares their stories and what was most important to them

Objects That Remind Us of Our Childhood

Most of us had favorite toys that influenced our lives in certain ways. In my case, it is the stuffed monkey (his name was Kofeeko) that my *savta* gave me when I was six years old and also Aurora, the giant doll (taller than me at the time) she brought to me from a trip to Spain. (Side note: Kofeeko and Aurora have now been "borrowed" by my daughter.) I created a list of my favorite childhood toys for my Box of Life and wrote a few words about what each meant to me. Both Kofeeko and Aurora have a special place.

I still remember the day when I was thirteen and my mom walked into my room to tell me it was time to get rid of my Barbie dolls. I panicked and planned how to hide them from her so I could play when she was not paying attention. I still have those dolls and many of their accessories saved in a box, and I've included one in my Box of Life. I love the idea that someday a descendant might say, "This is what my great-great-grandmother used to play with." With my Barbie there is a note explaining how playing with her helped me process many situations growing up—I worked through anxieties, family conflicts, dating, bullying, breakups, moves, and many other themes whenever I played Barbie with my friends Ofra in Ecuador or Dana in Colombia.

My friend Christopher keeps a pogo stick that he received for his eighth birthday—and even now in his fifties he still gets on it every once in a while. It reminds him of the joy he felt from receiving and mastering it and the freedom he felt bouncing from place to place. He has photos of himself on it then and now in his box.

Cecilia, a retired ESL teacher, told me, "I still have a few special objects from my childhood. One of them is a teddy bear named Charlie Brown. He reminds me of my childhood when I didn't have a lot of toys and was always happy with what I had."

Juan Carlos, also a teacher, heard our conversation about childhood memories and toys and shared, "One precious object for me is a wooden toy boat. It's small enough to fit in my pocket but robust enough to have survived many rough landings on the floor (and even the occasional bathtub dip). It's been polished by my hands over time, which adds to its beauty as well as its sentimental value—it feels like an old friend that I've grown up with. I'll never forget how excited I was when my parents gave it to me when I was nine years old for Christmas. They knew how much I loved boats, and they wanted me to have something special. And even though I don't play with it anymore, it sits on my desk and still reminds me of all the fun times we had together when I was little and thought nothing could ever go wrong in the world."

- Do you have any objects from your childhood? What made you keep these? Consider writing a few words about each one. What was your favorite thing about it? What did other people think about it? Was there something weird about it that made it unique or memorable?
- If you're boxing for a child, take a photo or video of them playing with their favorite toy. Create a timeline of the child's favorite toys and games over time.

Objects We Assign Special Powers To

The red ribbon in my purse for good luck, the bag with spices my mother-in-law gave me to put in my house for protection, my mom's prayer book on my nightstand, the ceramic angel my friends in Colombia gave me (which has been on my nightstand since I was ten) . . . you get the gist! I assign mystical power to objects, not the kind of power I assign to a higher power but more of a superstitious quality, one that can only help me feel better.

A friend of mine has what she calls her "magic yellow purse." She says it makes her feel confident and fabulous every time she uses it. It's made of yellow silk with golden embroidery and belonged to her grandmother, who once told her that every time she used to put her hand in it, she could feel the magic coming out. As a kid, my friend loved that story, and still to this day she chooses to believe there is some truth to it.

While getting my manicure done, the lady who was working on my nails told me she was having a challenging day. She shared, "I have a lucky charm that my uncle gave me. It's a small wooden elephant with a golden chain attached to it, and it has been around since before I was born. Whenever something bad happens or I feel like I'm having an unlucky day, I take out this little elephant and hold it in my hand until I feel better."

In my nightstand I keep a shell that a stranger gave to me once. It was a month after my dad passed and I was visiting Wrightsville Beach in North Carolina. The beach was one of my dad's favorite places, and I wanted to collect shells to take to the cemetery when I visited him. As I was strolling along the shore, a man with gray hair and bright-blue eyes stopped me and said, "Take this one; it is for you to keep. Lay it on your heart and you will

The shell

feel the strength of the ocean and its infinity. This shell is one of a kind and it is for you." Before I could say anything, the man vanished into the crowd. The encounter shook me, and that shell became the most special shell I could have ever imagined. In my mind, that man and that shell were sent to me by my dad to remind me of my own strength and the infinity of our love.

Reflect and Take Action

- Do you have any objects that you assign special powers to? What are they? How did they come to have their powers? How will they show up in your box?

Our Books

Books are powerful in their ability to suck us in, transport us to places we've never been, and introduce us to new ideas and perspectives. There are so many books that profoundly influenced who I am today. Self-help, autobiographical, and leadership books prevail on my bookshelves. I like books that inspire me to become the best version of myself. I also enjoy reading romance novels on a sunny day at the beach. There are a few books that I keep on my desk—ones that taught me concepts that I want to contemplate every single day.

In my box, I have a list of books I believe are a must-read for everyone, and in some cases, I've included a brief summary of the book and the impact it had on me.

I love to skim over the titles in people's libraries. It gives me a glimpse into their minds—what they're interested in, what they think is important. My friend Katrina loves historical fiction, and her shelves are full of novels about the past. She told me that she loves learning about history through the framework of a compelling story. My friend Allan is a college professor, and his shelves are full of books about psychology, attesting to his passion for understanding the human psyche. He wants to stay on top of any new concepts or theories in his field. And when it comes to my friend Anna, it is all about romance for her. She believes that books are an escape from her stressful job, and she wants something light and with happy endings.

I can't remember my *aba* without a book in his hands. Even after he lost his ability to read in the last nine months of his life, whenever I asked him what he was doing, he would answer, "Reading." I'm sure in his mind, he was reading. For him books were a source of wisdom. He would read every book more than once, each time uncovering new meaning and focusing on different aspects of what the author was conveying. My dad had many friends, and his books belonged to that group. He told me that as long as he had a book in his hands, he never felt lonely or bored.

My friend Joanne told me that she was including in her box a picture of the first page of the first book she purchased as a kid, along with an explanation. The book was *The Cat in the Hat* by Dr. Seuss. "About a year after the book was published in 1957, when I started to learn to read, I longed for my own copy. My father took me to the local stationery store next to the bakery where he always bought doughnuts for us on Sundays. He gave me one dollar and sent me out to buy the book. I met him back in the car with his change from my purchase. On the short trip home, I opened the book to the first page to start reading. But I was perplexed and unhappy with the large blue T in the first word, *The*. I suppose I had never seen a letter like that, especially since all the other letters looked normal to me. After complaining to my father that the book was "broken," I pitched it into the front seat and angrily said I didn't want it. My father said we were going to keep it and gave me a doughnut to calm me down. I did calm down and eventually read the book many times to myself and my little brother. Even then I must have had strong ideas about book layouts and designs that have stuck with me for over sixty years!"

"What are you reading?" is a question that many of us have probably been asked at some point in our lives. It's usually because the questioner wants to get to know us better. "What books are you commemorating in your Box of Life?" is a question we can start asking ourselves.

Reflect and Take Action

- Write a list, record yourself, or take a photograph of ten books that have influenced you. Briefly explain the impact they had on you and why.

> *"Books are the plane and the train and the road. They are the destination, and the journey. They are home."*
> —Anna Quindlen

Our Art

Like our books, the art we choose to display is personal and revealing. And often it means a lot to us. My husband's uncle and aunt have a home full of art that they've collected throughout their lifetime. My husband's ninety-six-year-old uncle walked us through every piece they own, telling us who the artist was, how they met, what the artist was conveying in the piece, and what it evokes in them. His art is one of his primary concerns when evaluating whether, when, and where to move or downsize in the future. His art is part of who he is and what gives him pleasure in life—it's part of his life story.

What do you choose to display in your home? What does it say about you? What pieces are most important to you and why?

Is Less More?

There is currently a shift toward valuing experiences over material things. The sharing economy encourages us to borrow or rent rather than own. Our books, photo albums, and music are moving from our shelves into a cloud. Shelly, in her fifties, shared an interesting perspective with me: "I think people of my grandparents' generation saved and valued things, despite not having much. My parents' generation, not so much. I think it's more and more common to throw things away in favor of having no things. We are constantly trading up to newer and better. This generation of our children seems to be more focused on experiences and less on stuff, so it will be even more important to figure out a way to save memories in concrete ways that can be passed on."

When my colleague Cecilia was downsizing for an upcoming move, she had a hard time getting rid of what she considered her "sentimental clutter." She acknowledged she had many things that "no longer served a purpose," which she had been collecting over the last thirty-seven years. She invited me to come over to help her decide what to keep, what to include when downsizing for her Box of Life, and what to get rid of . . . not an easy task, considering that most of the things she was looking at held sentimental value. Among the objects she had to decide on were the vase her first boyfriend gave her with flowers on their first anniversary, the broken ceramic dish she used every Christmas for big gatherings, and a collage her best childhood friend gave her in second grade. We agreed that for the items she would part with, she would first take a picture and write a description of the memory and emotion that it evoked. That photo and the description would go into her Box of Life at the end of the process. We also did some research to help us come up with two questions that could guide our decisions:

- What is significant about this item? Only if you can remember why you kept it this long and only if it evokes *positive* emotions may you keep it. If you can't remember, or it doesn't conjure positive emotions, pass it along to someone in the family who wants it, or donate it.
- Are you only keeping the object out of guilt or because you think it is the right thing to do for some other meaningful reason? If it is the former, see if someone else in the family wants it. If no one does, donate it.

Cecilia struck a good balance of things she would move to the new house, ones that went into her box, and ones that she would give away. I can't say the process was easy, as her emotions were all over the place, but at the end of it she said, "Less is more. I'm feeling so much lighter now that I'm ready to soar."

———

So, what objects could tell the story of your life? So often we stop seeing our possessions. Maybe it's time to take a good look at what you have and try to articulate its meaning to you. You may discover that you own some things you really don't care about and don't need. You may also discover that there are objects you didn't realize that you cherished. For these, take time to write down why they're meaningful and start planning how they will make an appearance in your Box of Life.

"You can't put a price on a sentimental value."
—Astrid Yrigollen

Chapter 14

Sharing Our Lessons

"The beautiful thing about learning is that nobody can take it away from you."
—B.B. King

We learn as we live. Moving through life, our experiences teach us lessons that we apply and share. Some of these lessons come easily; others are hard won. But all of us have some sage advice to share. In building our Box of Life, the story of our life will take center stage, and our life lessons will certainly play a role.

Learning from the Past

Although I'm a firm believer that personal experience is the best teacher and we need to learn our own lessons via the consequences of our actions, I also believe that learning from others is a gift. History must act as our guide and teacher. It can serve as an antidote to the lacking memory our society often reveals.

Being aware of what's happened in the past and the many transitions that have altered our trajectory helps me gain hope when I'm wondering about the direction the world is heading. History has taught me that at different times, great leaders emerged and accomplished what seemed impossible. Martin Luther King Jr. is an example I use when coaching executives about leadership and vision. History has also taught me that each one of us must follow Mahatma Gandhi's wise advice and "be the change [we] want to see in the world." No matter how insignificant we feel, we are all part of this world and have an influence. History isn't just a series of big, global events; it's what's happening around us. It's personal.

In my dad's Box of Life, I found an old cursive letter handwritten in Spanish on a thin, yellow piece of paper, dated August 12, 1949. It was a letter my grandparents sent him just after he had left Buenos Aires and set sail (yes, sail!) to Israel. It's mainly about how proud they were of him for going to study in Israel, bidding him to be responsible and take care of himself, and asking him to write home often. But what struck me the most was an altered version from the "Serenity Prayer" by Reinhold Niebuhr: "With serenity accept the things you cannot change, with courage change the things you can change, and with wisdom know the difference." My dad said those words to me since I was a little girl, but I'd never known that he'd learned them from his father and mother, who wrote them to him in a 1949 letter that I am able to hold in my hands today.

For my dad's memorial service, I prepared some words in his honor. I had already included this passage even before I found the letter in his box. Finding it only confirmed the true weight of this lesson on understanding what we can change versus what we must accept. The lesson has also served me well as I grieve my dad's loss. I'm forced to have the serenity to accept what I can't change: his passing.

The letter remains in my dad's box, but I've made a copy that is now in mine—it's a lesson from my grandparents to my dad and from my dad to me, and one that I share with my children as well.

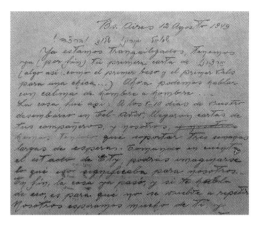

Excerpt from the letter my grandparents wrote to my dad in 1949

Bs. Aires 12 Agosto 1949

"Shmuel Yekareinu Shalom U'berachah" [Del Hebreo: Samuel nuestro querido, Paz y Bendiciones]

Ya estamos tranquilizados. Tenemos ya (por fin) tu primera carta de artzeinu. (algo así como el primer watlz para una chica . . .) Ahora podemos hablar con calma de hombre a hombre . . .

La cosa fue que a los diez días de vuestro desembarco en Tel Aviv, llegaron cartas de tus compañeros y nosotros hemos tenido que soportar tres semanas largas de esperar. Tomando en cuenta el estado de Ety, podrás imaginarte lo que esto significaba para nosotros. En fin, la cosa ya pasó, y si te hablo de eso es para que no se vuelva a repetir. Nosotros esperamos mucho de tí.

English Translation

Buenos Aires, August 12, 1949

"Shmuel Yekareinu Shalom U'berachah" [From Hebrew: Samuel, our precious one, Peace and Blessings]

We are finally reassured. We have received your first letter from our artzeinu [Hebrew for "our land"]—something like the first waltz dance for a girl . . . Now we can calmly talk man to man . . .

The thing was that ten days after your arrival in Tel Aviv, letters from your friends arrived, and we had to endure three long weeks of waiting. Considering Ety's pregnancy, you can imagine what this meant for us. Anyway, that time has passed, and I'm mentioning it so that it doesn't happen again. We have high hopes for you.

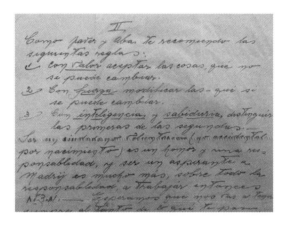

. . . *Como javer y aba [amigo y padre] te recomiendo las siguientes reglas:*

1) Con Valor aceptar las cosas que no se pueden cambiar.

2) Con Fuerza modificar las que sí se pueden cambiar.

3) Con Inteligencia y Sabiduría distinguir las primeras de las segundas.

Ser un ciudadano y voluntario (no accidental por nacimiento) es un honor y una responsabilidad, y ser un aspirante a Madrij, es mucho más sobre todo la responsabilidad . . .

English Translation

. . . As an *aba* and *javer* [Hebrew for "father and friend"], I recommend the following rules:

1) Courageously accept the things that cannot be changed.

2) With strength change the things that can be changed.

3) With intelligence and wisdom, distinguish the former from the latter.

Being a citizen and a volunteer (not by accident of birth) is an honor and a responsibility, and being an aspiring *Madrij* [Hebrew for "counselor"] is even more so, especially the responsibility . . .

Reflect and Take Action

- What life lessons have you learned during your life? When did you learn them, and from whom? How do these lessons impact your present? Create a timeline of lessons.

- Jot down a list of local, national, or world events that you believe had an impact on your life. What did they teach you?

- Think about the challenges you have faced and the impact they have had in your life. What did you lose or gain? What did you learn?

- What are five life lessons you want to pass on to your descendants? What can they learn from your missteps and successes?

- Consider including and completing the following sentence for every lesson of your life: "After I experienced _____, the most important lesson I learned was _____."

Sources of Learning

I asked a group of people who were boxing to think about which sources they attribute to the lessons they learned, other than their friends, family, teachers, and mentors. Some of the answers included the following:

- playing sports
- taking risks
- failing or succeeding
- community engagement
- vulnerabilities
- reading
- history
- life itself

Think about what activities have taught you the most. You might be surprised by what you discover.

Charles's Lessons

Charles had no shortage of wisdom or lessons to share. Our friendship nurtured my soul and mind, and there is no better testimony to that than the fact that I'm writing this book and giving birth to the Box of Life Project. The following are some of Charles's life lessons that deeply resonated with me, beyond the many other lessons already presented throughout the pages of this book.

Practice gratitude. Charles kept quotes and stories in his box reminding us that "there is always something to be thankful for and a reason to live." He took a few minutes every day to reflect and consider what he was thankful for that happened that day. Even on relatively straightforward days when nothing notable occurred, he could still always come up with plenty of things: a stranger with whom he broke bread, a good conversation, a smile from someone, fresh, home-baked cookies, doctors, etc. He said, "I even try to be thankful for the challenges that I encounter as I go along. Often, these are the things that present the biggest opportunity for growth, so why not be thankful?"

I adopted Charles's approach to gratitude. Gratitude is not a blindly optimistic or naive approach to life in which the "bad" things are ignored or whitewashed. It's more a matter of where we put our focus and finding a balance that can help us move forward with hope. The practice of gratitude as a tool for maintaining well-being has been popular for years. Unfortunately, we are trained to notice what is broken, undone, or lacking in our lives, so for many of us, gratitude remains a *practice* we have to consciously adopt.

When I'm working with my clients interpreting their performance reviews, I often find that they focus solely on areas for improvement and what's not working. I remind them that weaknesses and strengths usually come in pairs, one as an outcome of the other. When concentrating on our strengths and what we can do more of, we can overcome most of our areas that need development. When we practice giving thanks for what we have, instead of complaining about what we lack, we are giving ourselves an opportunity to create a new habit and the chance to experience all of life's gifts as blessings. By making a habit of gratitude, we no longer require special occasions to feel joy. We automatically become more aware of the good that happens to us and around us every day. The truth is, the simple fact that we are alive and able to experience *anything* is already *something* to be thankful for.

Reflect and Take Action

- List ten things you're grateful for. Keep that list where you can see it and add to it.
- Practice finding the hidden blessings in challenging situations or when you feel like complaining. Create a gratitude list (or even a gratitude journal), and you may be amazed by how much better you feel about yourself and your circumstances.

Be prepared for what you want. Charles's box had newspaper clippings about futuristic visions and possibilities. He spoke about what skills would be necessary in the future to avoid being left behind. "New opportunities will arise; if you remain ready, you won't miss the boat," is a quote from Charles in one of the interviews I found in his box. He believed we always need to be ready for the known and the unknown, or the "just in case," as he referred to it.

It breaks my heart when someone tells me, "I'm not ready for X, although X is what I always wanted." Generally, these statements are wrapped in excuses, tricking our minds into keeping us dormant in our comfort zone, holding us hostage from our true potential. I find my clients getting comfortable when they say, "I'm not ready," without realizing that their comfort zone will inevitably become their uncomfortable zone after staying stuck ceases to serve them. When you know what you want or know what's inevitably coming, no matter how far on the horizon it may be, prepare yourself so you don't miss the boat when it arrives. So often the things that seem endlessly far away are suddenly knocking on our door.

Being prepared will make a desired experience possible, easier, and better. It is about preventing excuses, lack of motivation, or procrastination from postponing what we want.

Reflect and Take Action

- What do you want to be prepared for? What do you need to do to get prepared?
- What opportunities did you have to let go of in the past because you were unprepared?

Be persistent but be flexible in how you pursue your goals. Persistence was a common denominator in Charles's box and his life. At times, Charles's persistence could be perceived as stubbornness. He was very articulate about what he wanted and how he wanted it, insisting until he either got his way or he realized it was truly impossible to accomplish. I seldom saw him give up, and when he had to, his frustration was palpable, but at least he found peace in knowing that he gave it his best. Very rarely did I hear him say, "I was wrong," and while I think he probably should have admitted those words more often, at least he lived his life in a consistently persistent way.

Whenever I pursued something, Charles would advise me to remember the definition of insanity: doing the same thing over and over again and expecting different results. If you're not getting the outcome you want, you must shift perspectives and try to approach the problem from a different angle. Change the story you are telling yourself if you want to change the output. This is an important tool I use in coaching.

When it comes to persistence, on one side of the spectrum we find those who give up as soon as they encounter the smallest roadblock. The opposite extreme are those who never give up, even after they've read a clear message on the wall that what they are trying to accomplish won't work. Being persistent is a positive personality trait, but like everything in life, it only works if it comes with the flexibility to change approaches.

Reflect and Take Action

- Can you think of three goals that you conquered because you were persistent? Can you think of three situations in which you were just "stubborn"?

Notice! Charles's box included a radio talk show proposal he wrote titled "People, Places & Proverbs." He described it as "people you pass but never notice, places you look at but never see, and proverbs submitted by people who changed their lives." Reading this inspired me to be more aware and regard people and places with extra curiosity and intent.

Mid-pandemic, my husband and I volunteered at a COVID-19 vaccination clinic as educators and Spanish interpreters. Because of a minor elbow surgery, my husband wore a sling. Some people noticed the sling and made remarks like "What happened to you?" or "Thank you for volunteering while recovering," while others ignored the obvious and simply listened to what my husband said without paying attention to the human being in front of them. I thought about Charles and took notice of those who took the time to connect and show some empathy toward my husband, if even briefly, and of those who just passed by.

Noticing is about awareness, being present in the moment, connecting with your surroundings, and paying attention to what you see. You might be surprised by the doors you can open just by noticing, and how your world will expand.

Reflect and Take Action

- Take a moment to pause and really look at your surroundings. You may be amazed at what's there that you didn't notice before. Consider starting a "Today I noticed . . ." journal to hone your perception skills. Choose a few entries to include in your box.

The details are what truly make the difference. By now, you should have a good idea of how detail-oriented Charles Stern was. He thought of every detail, down to how his legacy and wisdom would live on once he was physically gone. Many of the stories inside Charles's box echoed the importance of details.

Just as he and I shared many other personality traits, we

also shared an attention to detail. We enjoyed speaking about details that could elevate an experience. Details are what make the difference in how we make people feel and what they will remember and pass on to other generations.

I remember one Mother's Day when my kids were in elementary school and I received two pencil holders as gifts—one from my daughter's class and one from my son's class. Both were lovely, but one of them was complete with many details, while the other one appeared unfinished. I knew it was the teacher who urged my child to keep working on the pencil holder, paying attention to every tiny detail, and by doing so, she modeled how to complete a project.

I always remind my clients that it's not just about presenting a report; it's about how you present it and the details behind it that will distinguish you from the rest. Details show care, dedication, contemplation, and that you are aware of the whole picture, not just some of the smaller pieces. Details set apart the ordinary from the extraordinary, they can transform any situation into a memorable one, and they can elevate every lived experience. Use them well. Attention to detail is always a good thing.

Reflect and Take Action

- What details do you need to think about to make your box memorable?

Knowledge is different from wisdom, but both are important. I found a newspaper clipping in Charles's box in which he was quoted saying, "You know everything there is to know about the topic, but now use only your wisdom to make a recommendation." Wisdom is what converts the knowledge into breakthroughs. During one of our many conversations, Charles explained that wisdom is about knowing which facts are relevant and why they're relevant. "Wisdom encompasses knowledge, experience, a good dose of emotional intelligence, and active listening," he said in what I called his expert tone of voice.

I couldn't agree more: we need knowledge, and we should all work tirelessly to acquire it, but knowledge alone doesn't take us far if there is no wisdom along with it.

In my box, I'm including the lessons I've learned from the wise people I've met on my journey.

Reflect and Take Action

- Who are the wise people in your life? How will they make an appearance in your box?

Ask questions. From an early age, we learn about the world by asking questions. The depth of our lives is based on the questions we ask and on those questions we don't ask. Questions nourish us like water nourishes plants. The more we're watered, the more we grow.

Charles loved asking and receiving questions. He proposed challenging, thought-provoking queries that often had more than one right answer—the question itself was a gift. He pondered many philosophical issues as well as practical ones.

One of Charles's favorite questions was, "What if?" He even gave me a book from his library titled *What If?* In the book, a baby bird, whose mom is encouraging him to leave the nest, asks, "What if I fall?" She responds, "What if you fly?" We need to complete the "What if?" questions with questions that free us, not confine us. Self-limiting beliefs chain us to a heavy load that won't allow us to fly. Charles told me that I should always ask, "What if?" before saying "No" to anything. "What if?" became my favorite question of all time, and thanks to it I became brave enough to write this book. I asked myself, "What if, regardless of all the reasons why I shouldn't write this book in English, I still do it, and even if it isn't a literary masterpiece, the lessons from Charles touch a few people's lives?"

Reflect and Take Action

- Create a list of ten questions that remain unanswered for you to this day. One of the questions on my list is: Why don't we always do what we know is the right thing to do for ourselves and for others? Include your list in your box.

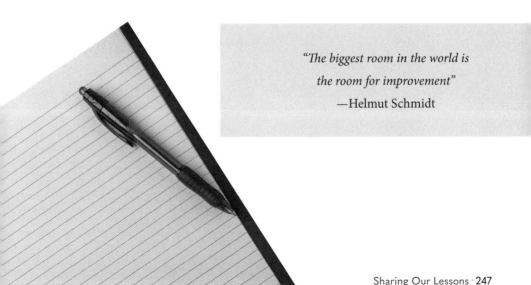

> "The biggest room in the world is
> the room for improvement"
> —Helmut Schmidt

Early Wisdom

You don't need to live a long life to learn a lot from your time on this earth. After three years of major life transitions and growth and just before her twenty-fifth birthday, Zoe started compiling twenty-five items she wanted to share with her friends, family, and especially the young women in her life. Below is a sample of the list she shared on social media with the people in her life, a list that Zoe already boxed. For the full list, please visit The Box of Life Project website at www.oritramler.com/zoes-list/.

Lessons I've learned in my twenty-five years:

1. Eat the damn cookie.
2. Listen to your body's signals.
3. Stop apologizing for taking up space, for using your voice, for articulating what you want.
4. When you witness racism, sexism, anything-ism—call bullshit.
5. Take a minute and breathe. Life is already too fast; no need to speed it up.
6. Start going to therapy. Even when you feel fine, build that support system.
7. Three to five really close friends are infinitely more valuable than thirty to fifty surface-level friends.
8. Apologize sincerely.
9. Bottling up your feelings does nothing but crack the bottle until it explodes.
10. Know your worth and don't be afraid to walk away from those who don't recognize it.

My Next Decade Manifesto

Like Zoe, an impending birthday inspired me to focus on what I'd learned and what mattered to me most. Facing fifty, I realized I finally felt at home in my own skin! I felt stronger, more confident, wiser, more fulfilled, and more grounded than I had in decades past. I learned many things during my first five decades, and based on those, I committed to a few resolutions, which I shared with the world in a blog post. Those fifty resolutions are in my Box of Life, and I plan to update them every ten years . . . or less. Here are ten of them. Visit The Box of Life Project at www.oritramler.com/my-next-decade-manifesto/ for the full list.

1. I will make each day count. I've learned that one year equals 365 opportunities and what we do every day matters more than what we do occasionally.

2. I will start going through my bucket list and visit beautiful landscapes, rent a house on the beach, paint while listening to the waves, and take naps and walks on the sand as often as I can. I've learned that I need to do more of what makes me feel good and spend more time in my "happy places."

3. I will trust my intuition and gut. I've learned to respect my inner voice.

4. I will have the courage to live a life true to myself. I will say what I think and stop agreeing with other people when I actually disagree with them. No more nodding my head *yes* when I'm thinking *no*. I've learned that each of our unique ways of thinking is priceless, and that's what makes the world wiser and more interesting.

5. I will always have a project to look forward to. I've most likely lived more years than I have left to live, and I still have much to do. I've learned to be thankful that I haven't accomplished everything I desire. If I did, what would there be to look forward to?

6. I will surf through life, as I've learned that I can't control the waves.

7. I will have more fun and nurture my inner child, let loose, and be sillier more often. I've learned that you need to plan for fun; it doesn't just happen.

8. I will let all my angels know who they are. I will tell those who changed or influenced me in various wonderful ways how they impacted me. I've learned that oftentimes we say or do something that changes someone else forever without even being aware of it.

9. I will create more romantic and magical moments. I've learned that love requires dedication and care, and that romance brings a special spark to life.

10. I will remind myself that two people can look at the same thing and see it completely differently. I've learned that I need to be curious and learn from what others see and have to say.

What are the lessons you've learned over the course of your life? Have you had the opportunity to express and share them? Over the next few weeks, try to keep these questions top of mind and see what comes up.

Reflect and Take Action

- Knowing what you know now, what advice would you have given to yourself in the past? Write a letter to your younger self to include in the box.

Chapter 15

Adversities and Roads Not Taken

"Vulnerability sounds like truth and feels like courage. Truth and courage aren't always comfortable, but they are never weakness."

—Brené Brown

Have you ever met anyone who had no obstacles to overcome? No setbacks or moments of self-doubt? No anxieties? The Box of Life is not about capturing a flawless, free-of-pain, utopic, happy life. If that were the case, then the box would be a poor representation of reality. Life is a rich palette of dark moments, bright moments, and moments of every shade in between. In Charles's box I found a full spectrum of colors. Because of his intensity and passion, life for him was a colorful canvas of emotions and experiences.

I found troubling medical reports and newspaper clips detailing his battles with severe illnesses. I found rejection letters telling him he wasn't good enough and letters notifying him that he was no longer wanted at his job. I found lists of all the things he pursued without success. Most importantly, however, I found a few of his writings reflecting on what he had learned from each adversity he faced. It was a real person's box, not one of fantasy. "I'm not afraid of criticism or rejection—if I don't achieve my goal, it is because I haven't tried hard enough or I took the wrong steps," Charles said in an article I found in his box. After all, there is no such thing as a perfect life, but there is growth as a result of our losses, failures, tribulations, and disappointments.

Remember William Shakespeare's words, "No legacy is so rich as honesty." Be honest while building your Box of Life and don't make things seem better or worse than they were. Humans relate to other humans, and humans are not perfect. Your imperfect, vulnerable aspects are what make you interesting and relatable.

Don't Fear the Wind

Charles was very elastic; he re-created himself repeatedly, and flexibility was an attribute he believed in. When I faced a challenge with a donor for our organization, Charles reminded me to be flexible and realize that there is more than one approach to any situation. He encouraged me to learn from the trees, saying, "If they were rigid, the wind would break them, yet due to their flexibility, they remain intact and move with grace at the highest of winds. Similarly," he continued, "planes take off and land against the wind, and kites also propel against the wind." Perhaps trees, planes, and kites can teach us a lesson—we should not fear the winds of adversity but rise with them.

During the COVID-19 pandemic, I found myself sharing that same advice with my clients. I reminded and encouraged them to remain flexible, to find new ways, and to rise with the winds.

Facing Adversity

Imagine life as one long run. The journey is not on a straight, flat, smoothly paved path; on the contrary, it is filled with hills, valleys, and intersections at every corner. During our journey we will get lost, make more than one U-turn, and even change our destination as we go. At times, the wind will blow hard against us, adding another layer of challenges.

As I've grown older, I've realized that we must not be afraid of temporarily falling apart, because only by being broken down can we rebuild. Breakthroughs usually happen when we hit rock bottom and we let our vulnerability show. A client who enjoys running once told me, "As a runner, my proudest moment is typically not after winning a race—it is after a strenuous climb that previously seemed unconquerable." He reminds himself of that feeling whenever he is facing challenges at the company he now leads.

In the face of adversity, we need to consider the following questions:

- How will we meet this adversity?
- What will we learn from it?
- What will we allow it to take away from us? What will we protect?
- How are we going to overcome it?
- What opportunities does it bring?

One time I tried to engage a community member to sponsor a big event—with no success—and Charles noticed my frustration. He reminded me that British Prime Minister Margaret Thatcher once said, "You may have to fight a battle more than once to win it." I laughed because, as I often mention, Charles was off-the-charts stubborn. He knew well how to fight until he got what he was looking for. I responded by citing Thomas A. Edison, who wisely said, "Every failure is a lesson learned about your strategy." Charles went on to say that if I still don't win after a few battles, I should learn from the salesman's wisdom: "In the sales world, you can expect one of two things to happen. People will either buy from you or will say no to you. No matter what the case is, you say thank you. If they say no, you move on to knock on the next door and make your next sale." To this day I recall that conversation every time I face frustration, and then I smile. I changed the strategy on how I approached that community member, and he wound up happily sponsoring the event with great pride.

Vulnerabilities and adversities are part of our story. I hope your Box of Life can reflect the fact that how you dealt with adversities mattered more than the adversities themselves, and that being vulnerable doesn't make you necessarily weak, but it certainly makes you human.

Reflect and Take Action

- Think about the challenges you have encountered and the impact they have had on your life. Create a timeline of challenges and the lessons you learned from them.
- Share three situations in which you had to be flexible. Did you succeed?
- Share five things that inspire you to keep going and explain why.
- What were five of the most embarrassing moments you ever experienced? What did you learn from those moments?
- Create a list of important experiences and stories that you consider "taboo" or are choosing *not* to include in your Box of Life. Explain why. Consider finding the courage to at least include that list in your box.

By the Way . . .

I once had a client named Dan. Dan was pursuing the next steps in his career, and as I was working on his intake form, I couldn't help but think how accomplished this young man was. He was looking for growth and more responsibilities, and he mentioned that his only condition was to work in a place with reliable public transportation. At the end of the intake form, I always ask if there is any other information my clients want to share with me that I hadn't asked already. His answer to that was, "By the way, I'm blind." With that brief statement, my client taught me that his blindness was not his defining trait. It wasn't his entire identity, and he didn't want to be known for it. It was more of a "by the way" thing. Charles and my client both knew that what really matters about our vulnerabilities is what we choose to do with them.

When I speak about vulnerability, I refer to the inability to withstand the impact of a hostile environment, or of an environment that we perceive as hostile. In such environments our defenses are diminished, compromised, or lacking. When we are vulnerable, we feel we can be easily hurt, influenced, or attacked. Vulnerability is part of being human, and it is not a bad thing as long as we acknowledge the emotion and use it to move forward.

I asked a number of people when they feel most vulnerable and how they deal with it. Here are some of their answers:

- When I'm being bullied by a coworker—I deal with it by letting my supervisor know and I stand up for myself.
- When I'm not in control of a situation—I'm still learning how to deal with it.
- When politicians make stupid decisions—my only response is to laugh.
- When nature shows its force—my house is next to the ocean. I do my best to be prepared for whatever comes my way.
- When I need to speak in public—it makes me feel naked in front of the room. I'm working with a coach and practicing meditation to help me feel grounded and calm.
- When I lost my job—I felt that my life was over. It took me a while to understand that what I lost was my job, not my life.
- When I lost my elderly mom to COVID-19—I joined a

support group and I'm trying my best to keep living my life, as she would want me to do.

- When I got rejected from my dream school—I ended up going to my backup choice and having the best experience I could hope for.

My neighbors Kruti and Mehul shared with me how they deal with adversity. They told me, "The concept of karma is deeply woven into the fabric of our culture. Karma implies an action or deed, not just immediate but also past and potentially in the future. Our belief states very firmly that our own karma will either help or hinder our progress in life—material as well as spiritual. A direct effect of this belief is to be careful with our own actions, which in turn leads to thoughtful action rather than acting on impulse. It also leads to a sense of acceptance for things which are not in our control. The literal thought process, when faced with unforeseen adversity, is that we must have done something in the past to get this result, so accept that it cannot be changed and move on creating better karma in life."

Adversity will meet us at certain points of our lives. It's not a question of *if* it will come but rather a question of *when* or *how* it will come. Many of the challenges we face are hard to overcome, and some have a long-lasting impact on the way we behave and live our lives. Having said that, it is important to remember that we are most likely built with coping skills to help us move forward, even when it seems impossible. There are resources we can reach out to, and it is important to know how to ask for help no matter how hard that can be.

Reflect and Take Action

- Recall moments of adversities and times when you felt vulnerable in your life. How did you cope and how did you handle them?

- Include in your box rejection letters, important medical records, and documents of all sorts that share obstacles, losses, and challenges that you had to overcome.
- Reframe failures and rejections into affirmations. For example: "I didn't get into X school, and thanks to that rejection, I got into Z school, where I met my future wife." Or "I was let go from my job, and thanks to that, I'm now in a much healthier working environment."

Charles and Adversity

I had a good laugh when I found in Charles's box what I later learned is probably an urban myth known as a rejection letter from a publisher. It reads: "We have read your manuscript with boundless delight. If we were to publish your book, it would be impossible for us to publish any work of lower standard. And as it is unthinkable that, in the next thousand years, we shall see its equal, we are, to our regret, compelled to return your divine composition and to beg you a thousand times to overlook our short sight and timidity."

When any of Charles's proposals were rejected, he found a way to put a smile on his face and still feel good about himself, a personality trait that I admire.

Charles taught me that when adversity shows up at our doorstep, we can find meaning in our struggles. Focusing on this meaning can help us find the motivation to move forward. I've realized that I have a hard time tolerating people who get stuck in one place or in one emotion. As Winston Churchill said, "If you are going through hell, keep going." I do my best to help clients do exactly that.

I remember a time a client was going through a tough time at work. After listening to him vent for a few minutes, I asked him to pause and take a deep breath. It was clear that he was facing serious challenges, but I reminded him that these challenges presented an opportunity for him to grow and define himself as a leader. I was very pleased when he nodded, paused, and quoted

Albert Einstein: "Adversity introduces man to himself." Our reaction to the challenge we are facing is as important as the challenge itself.

Letting Go

While I was describing boxing to my friend Cynthia, she shared her belief that "the Box of Life should also be about the things we choose not to pursue, all the things that we let go of throughout our journey." I found Cynthia's idea intriguing, recognizing that what we decide not to include in our boxes—the things we deem unimportant, the choices we don't want others to find out about, and the opportunities we didn't explore—is also revealing and worth exploring.

One of the hardest things to do is let go. Whether it is letting go of love, dreams, loss, betrayal, anger, or guilt, change is never easy.

Three things came to mind as I reflected on "letting go." The first was about opportunities that we embrace versus those that we pass up. The second was about letting go of behaviors, unhealthy thoughts, fears, and habits that hold us back. And the third was about grudges we hold for too long, ghosts from the past who continue to haunt us, and unhealthy relationships or feelings that we continue to cultivate.

> **The Road Not Taken.** The first thought I had during my conversation with Cynthia was that we are just as defined by the opportunities we pass up as we are by those we choose to pursue. In our boxes, most of us wouldn't likely think to include those times we were offered a great job but turned it down because it seemed too demanding, or the title of the book we never wrote, or person we dread to ask out because of fear or lack of motivation. But I think we should. What we actively choose *not* to do is important and defines what's next for us in life.
>
> I have three things that I let go of that somehow defined my life for better or for worse. They all played a significant role in

setting my path, and thus they are worthy of being in my box. The first one was when I turned eighteen and was suddenly old enough to get drafted to the Israeli Defense Force. I was living in Argentina, and my parents convinced me that being an only child and ready to start college were two good reasons to request an exemption and not serve. I remember thinking, How can I turn my back on my duty as an Israeli citizen? For a long time I regretted listening to my parents, and I am still convinced the skills I could have gained would have served me well for the rest of my life. At the same time, by staying where I was, I met my husband, and many good things followed.

The second thing I let go of was my desire to become a psychiatrist. I was influenced both by my personal fear of embarking on a challenging career and by my parents' lack of encouragement. To this day, I regret not pursuing a medical career, although at the same time I have no regrets about how everything turned out in my life after that decision.

The last thing I let go of was not having more children. I have two amazing kids, and when we moved to the United States, they were one and five years old. The move was already a big transition for us, and I was scared I wouldn't be able to provide everything for them that I wanted to give while they were so far away from family and familiarity. I figured it would be even more difficult if I had another child. In hindsight, I was wrong.

I let go of all those "What if?" thoughts and regrets because I believe we can't second-guess our decisions by looking back at them from our current vantage point; we can only judge them based on the information we had when they originally occurred. At the time they took place I was doing the best I could. Remember, I believe that everything happens for a reason.

If I hadn't had the conversation with Cynthia, those three

stories would probably not have appeared in my box. Now I'm reevaluating how important it is to include things that didn't come to fruition because of our own choices. What Charles chose not to include in his box is something only he will ever know.

Life presents us with opportunities that we often ignore, choose not to pursue, or perhaps aren't even aware of. These decisions have a long-term compounding effect on the rest of our journeys and thus should be considered as important as those things which we do pursue and accomplish.

Reflect and Take Action

- What are five things you could have pursued that you ignored or didn't engage with? How have those decisions impacted your life in the long term? Which ones are you sharing in your Box of Life, and which ones will remain unknown?
- What was the most painful or difficult thing you had to let go of, and why? How did you feel after you let go of it?

Baggage. Let's look into the second thought that came out of my conversation with Cynthia: letting go of behaviors that hold us back.

We need to let go of things that happened to us in the past that are holding us back from living fully in the present. That was clearly one of Charles's strengths. Rather than dwell on insecurities and bitter experiences, he directed his focus to trying new things that were of interest to him. We can't change the past, but we can decide how we live in the present and try to plan for our future. Our past can inform and enrich our future, but it does not define it; instead, our actions today will define who we become. Charles was always building upon the challenges he confronted, and if one thing didn't turn out as expected, to the next thing he would turn.

I must confess that people who get stuck in their emotions, ruminate about the same things of the past, or live with excuses tend to frustrate me. Getting stuck is a choice, and although it is true that many people don't know how to keep moving forward and could use some help, it still disheartens me. Too often, what bothers us becomes our comfort zone—we complain about it and use it as an excuse but make no effort to change the situation.

My coaching client BJ shared that when he returned to his childhood home in Wisconsin to attend the funeral of his father, he put together a box containing his dad's most precious belongings, as well as notes and drawings his dad made during his long, debilitating illness before he died. BJ also jotted down moments he and his dad shared together, inspired by photos he found that his father had kept. As BJ put the box together, he realized he had to let go of some painful memories of his father's unhealthy behaviors in order to move forward with his own life and forgive his dad for not being the person BJ needed him to be. Creating his dad's box helped him remember that they also had shared valuable moments together, which was a good way of letting go of the shadows in their relationship.

I'm choosing to include a list of my unhealthy habits and behaviors in my box, and I explain how I overcame them or did not. Most importantly, I'm also explaining the consequences of my behaviors. You might be wondering what they are . . .

- Drinking too much Coca-Cola (overcame successfully)
- Not exercising (still working on that one)

- Looking at my cell phone before going to sleep (not sure I can succeed on changing that one but trying)
- Paying too much attention to my own wishes on how others should behave in life instead of accepting them as they are, without judgment or expectation (still trying to find the right balance on this one)

It is a skill to know what we need to let go of so we don't remain attached to heavy loads that keep us stuck. Life will continue regardless of whether we hold a self-pity party, move forward, or stay put. As Carl Jung said, "I am not what happened to me, I am what I choose to become."

Reflect and Take Action

- Are there any behaviors or emotions that are holding you back? Are you stuck in any way? What ideas do you have to get yourself unstuck?
- What three things do you need to let go of? What benefit will letting go bring?

Forgiveness. My third thought when speaking with Cynthia was about forgiveness—of others and ourselves. Forgiveness often requires courage, strength, and a decent dose of humility. We need to let go of unhealthy relationships, and that includes releasing any grudges. When we forgive, we do it for ourselves as much as for the person we are forgiving.

Forgiveness can involve accepting a heartfelt apology. When someone has taken the time to reconsider an unkind word or action and offers an apology, I believe we must make every attempt to accept it graciously. Maturity is recognizing that we aren't perfect. When we forgive, we grow in stature. We show our realization that we, too, can make a hurtful or hateful mistake.

Sometimes you have to forgive those who haven't apologized or made amends. Holding onto the hurt is simply not worth it. As American advice columnist Ann Landers said, "Hanging on to resentment is letting someone you despise live rent-free in your head." Forgiveness is liberating.

I once read about a concept that I will always remember, but, ironically, I can't remember where I read it. The author explained that forgiveness is the power of giving love from you and to you; forgiving is for *giving*, not for *taking*. By giving mercy to others, you give mercy to yourself.

Perhaps one of the most difficult decisions my family and I had to make recently was accepting the fact that it was time to provide my dad with hospice care. I felt as if I were disappointing him, letting go of him, giving up on any ounce of remaining hope. My friend Dr. Jonathan Fischer, MD, a hospice and palliative medicine specialist at Duke University Hospital, listened to my pain and reminded me how important it was to provide comfort and quality of life to my dad at this stage. Our conversations enabled me to let go of what used to be and to welcome the new reality. Was it scary to accept that there were no more treatments to make my dad better and to face the fact that the end of his life was coming? Of course it was! However, by preventing countless more trips to the hospital and painful interventions, I was also telling him how much I loved him. Letting go can break us at the first moment, but holding on can break us forever.

Reflect and Take Action

- Who do you need to forgive in order to move forward?
- Who have you forgiven in the past and how do you feel about it?
- What do you want to be forgiven for?
- What are some of your regrets?

The Five Remembrances

I found Buddhism's Five Remembrances in Charles's box. Over 2,500 years ago, Buddha taught his monks to recite them every morning so that they would be grounded in what is true and real: Everything is impermanent. We have and own nothing but our actions. We repair their consequences from moment to moment, from lifetime to lifetime.

I am of the nature to grow old. There is no way to escape growing old.
I am of the nature to have ill health.
There is no way to escape ill health.
I am of the nature to die. There is no way to escape death.
All that is dear to me and everyone I love are of the nature to change.
There is no way to escape being separated from them.
My actions are my only true belongings. I cannot escape the consequences of my actions. My actions are the ground upon which I stand.

Buddha's teaching is a good reminder that illness, aging, and death are all parts of the natural order. The only things we can control are our actions and how we react to events around us. As I was reading the last line of the passage, I realized that our Box of Life is also grounding: it serves as a clear reflection of our actions and their consequences. Our box transcends all life cycles.

Letting Go Is a Skill

My neighbor and friend Parkavi, a child and adolescent psychiatrist, shared the following insight with me: "I let go of a few things that were very important to me. To begin with, I let go of living in my country, as I did not see a future for me and my boyfriend (now husband). I feared that somehow I would be separated from him due to family traditions and expectations. I let go of life in the United Kingdom to move to the United States, which is where my boyfriend saw a brighter future for us (though I hate to say it, he was right). I let go of my residency at the prestigious Mayo Clinic in Rochester, Minnesota, because I did not want to be in a long-distance relationship with my soon-to-be husband and instead took a residency spot where he got one. I let go of anger and resentment because I did not like who it was turning me into. I let go of expecting others to be part of my dream, as I realized they have dreams of their own. I am learning to let go of my tight hold around my kids, as they are turning into teenagers and learning to fly high on their own. I have to say that last one is the hardest, as I still want to hold them next to me every second of my life, even in my dreams." Parkavi continues to inspire me with her thoughtful insights and approach to life. Like any other skill, we need to practice and exercise letting go, even if it is hard at times. As author and blogger Mandy Hale put it, "Growth is painful. Change is painful. But nothing is as painful as staying stuck somewhere you don't belong."

I've asked a group of people what they have learned after letting go of something and their answers included the following:

- I could trust again even though I was betrayed.
- I could have a healthy relationship even if I was in a toxic one before.
- I could tolerate being with someone who hurt me in the past and even like them a little.
- I could make good choices even if I made poor choices in the past.
- I could get my dream job even if I was fired before.

When we let go of something, we are making room for something else. To give way to new opportunities, we need to stop doing what does not serve us well.

Penelope is putting her Box of Life together, and she decided to include clippings of her dark brown hair that she collected from her stylist at her last haircut. She is preserving it in a Ziploc bag. She wrote, "I finally decided to stop coloring my hair and to let it grow out gray. I want my box to reflect that it is hard for me to let go of my youth, but I know it is inevitable no matter how much I try to hold on to it. By coloring my hair I've been holding on to an illusion. I will remain young in spirit and health, but I will let my body be who it is. This decision is liberating at least. I hope my box will remind me of both what I was and how lucky I am to see my life evolve and age. My mom passed when she was forty-seven; she didn't have the privilege to even think about her gray hair."

> *"When one door closes, another door opens; but we so often look so long and so regretfully upon the closed door, that we do not see the ones which open for us."*
> —Alexander Graham Bell

Reflect and Take Action

- Create a list of what you had to let go of and what you still need to let go of. What are you holding on to? What slows you down? What riles you up?

We are the curators of our lives as much as we are of our Boxes of Life, and we decide what we can let go of. As we go through life, some things from our past are going to become more relevant, and some will be less relevant. British singer Zayn Malik said it beautifully: "There comes a day when you realize turning the page is the best feeling in the world, because you realize there is so much more to the book than the page you were stuck on." As we look back into our Box of Life, it is okay to get rid of things that were once important and make room for others, just as we do in life.

"Sometimes letting go is an act of far greater power than hanging on."
—Eckhart Tolle

Chapter 16

Parting Words: The Box of Life Is a Lifelong Pursuit

"Ask yourself which traces you want to leave in this world, which message you want to live, and you will contact your true image . . ."

—Dr. Rosina-Fawzia Al-Rawi

Now that you've reached the end of this book, I hope I can officially welcome you into the boxing community. I also hope that I have fulfilled Charles's goal of letting the world know who Charles Morris Stern was, and that some of the insights shared through the pages of this book will influence your own Box of Life and help you live a more fulfilling life. Am I too ambitious with my expectations? Maybe, but one of the main lessons I learned from Charles was to always aim high.

Putting together your box gives you the authority to tell your story the way you want to be remembered, using your own voice—it's not determined by others. It also offers a sense of creating a lasting legacy. When approaching the end of his life, Charles had one main worry: "Will I be forgotten, Orit?" I responded, "No, you won't—I now have your Box of Life." Some other benefits of boxing include the following:

- serving as a compass to our values, what matters most to us, and how we want to live our lives
- passing on our life legacy and nurturing our roots
- having a resource that reduces memory loss by triggering memories
- calming anxiety by reminding ourselves of what we or others have overcome
- fostering a sense of belonging by reconnecting with our friends and loved ones through cherished memories
- providing comfort in times of grief and loss
- anchoring us in times of transitions
- creating a sense of community by being part of something greater than ourselves
- inspiring others with our life stories

I recommend storing your box—in whatever form it takes—in a place where you can access it *on demand*. You may find it helpful in times of tumult—it can serve as an anchor, filled with reminders from the past that can help us look forward into the future. Revisiting where we once were can be comforting and healing. If the past was better than today, it reminds us of the great times that no one can take away from us. If it was worse, it shows us that we were resilient and that we can overcome challenges.

Of course, boxing is a lifelong process. We have new experiences, thoughts, and accomplishments every day, and what matters to us changes over time. What was important once may not be as important anymore, if at all. Our priorities and outlook on life evolve and change, just like we evolve and change throughout our lives. Thus, boxing is an ongoing project, one that can last our entire lives.

As you continue curating your box and decide that there are things that are no longer relevant, you can put them somewhere else (such as a different physical box or digital file). That other place will not be your Box of Life per se, but it can still be a box of memories that occasionally you enjoy looking at, even if it would not be relevant to others.

The Joys of Unboxing

Think about what you feel every time you open a package, whether it's something you expect or it's a surprise. We wrap gifts not only to make them special and thoughtful, but to give the receiver the pleasure of anticipation.

If we can get that special feeling and excitement when opening a gift or product, just imagine the feeling we can get from unboxing a life. My experience unboxing Charles's and my parents' boxes is one that is hard to describe. I felt anticipation about what I would find and excitement over what I found. I felt the intrigue of wanting to learn more, the emotion of feeling their souls, and the joy of hearing stories that I would have missed if it hadn't been for these boxes.

Unboxing my dad's Box of Life evoked powerful emotions. While doing so I had to be extremely careful not to let any of my tears stain the yellowed, fragile paper treasures I was holding. I inhaled the smell of an old encyclopedia or historical archive as it came back to life again. Overall, the experience brought more smiles than tears, although the frustration of not having done the unboxing while I could ask my dad questions and enjoy it with him was hard to swallow.

There is pleasure and healing not only in putting the box together but also in the unboxing process. If someone opens your box a hundred years from now, what and who will they find?

"Surprise is the greatest gift which life can grant us."
—Boris Pasternak

One Last Invitation to Reflect and Take Action

- If you haven't already, start boxing now, and not for the number of *likes* and *followers*. Keep it honest and begin documenting, curating, and storing the pivotal moments in your life and the things that matter to you most. Chances are, someone else will benefit from what you create beyond the treasure that you will be making for yourself. Once in a while you will look back at what you've documented and gain new perspectives about your own life. Trust your heart and embrace the journey!

"Our own life has to be our message."
—Thich Nhat Hanh

A Version of "We Remember Them" by Sylvan Kamens and Rabbi Jack Riemer, Found in Charles's Box

In the rising of the sun and its going down,

We remember them;

In the blowing of the wind and the chill of winter,

We remember them;

In the opening of the buds and in the rebirth of spring,

We remember them;

In the rustling of leaves and in the beauty of autumn,

We remember them;

In the beginning of the year and when it ends,

We remember them;

When we are weary and in the need of strength,

We remember them;

When we are sick and lost at heart,

We remember them;

When we have joys and we yearn to share,

We remember them;

So long as we live, they too shall live, for they are part of us, as

We remember them.

from *The Gates of Repentance* prayer book

"*You may tell a tale that takes up residence in someone's soul,
becomes their blood and self and purpose. That tale will move them
and drive them, and who knows what they might do because of it,
because of your words. That is your role, your gift.*"
—Erin Morgenstern

Appendix 1

Boxing Cheat Sheet

B ased on my experience coaching individuals on creating their boxes, I've compiled an outline of steps to take during the process. I hope you find it helpful in getting you started. Please bear in mind that there is no single "right way" to box—do what works best for you. Remember that you can write things down or record or film yourself. Most important, don't constrain your creativity in any way.

1. Putting Together Your General Timeline

- Create a general timeline of your life. It can begin with your family history or with your birth.
- Include a few significant memories or milestones for the following categories, depending on what stage of life you are in:
    - earliest memories and childhood
    - teenage years

- early adult years
- middle adult years
- adult years
- senior years
- Include as much or as little as you'd like. You don't need to know or remember everything.

2. Deciding What's Important to You

- Think about what topics are important to you—for example, family, friends, work, values, life lessons. If you need inspiration for topics you might cover, see the list of categories on page 279. You can start boxing as many topics as you want. Alternatively, you can focus your boxing on life stages, milestones, or any other criteria that works for you. Start by labeling a folder or digital file for each category you are choosing.
- For the category that you are boxing, consider the following:
  - Create a timeline for that topic. It will likely be more specific than the general timeline you already have. For example, you can create a timeline covering your friendships, education, work, travel, values . . . the list goes on and on.
  - Create a list of your favorite or most impactful memories for each topic and explain why they're meaningful. Share the when, where, who, what, and why of those moments.
  - Are there any lessons learned that are worth sharing and that relate to each of the topics you are boxing? What wisdom was gained?
  - Are there any challenges that you have or have not overcome related to the topics you are boxing, and

what impact have they had in your life?

3. Bringing Your Stories to Life in Each Category

- Your photos: Select five to ten photos that you can add to enhance your timeline, lists, stories, or information. Label each photo with the when, where, who, what, and why.
- Your stuff: What ten mementos, documents, objects, letters, emails, cards, etc. do you have that are relevant for this category? If you prefer to stay digital, you can take pictures of anything physical and include those photos in the box, rather than the objects themselves. Label everything with the when, where, who, what, and why.

4. Continuing to Box

- Is there anything important missing from your box that could enhance or complete your life story in that category or clarify what matters most to you?
- As time goes on and you live new experiences and continue to evolve, don't forget to update your box accordingly.

Happy boxing!

Categories to Box

Figuring out what to include in your box can be overwhelming. This section includes a list of categories to consider, but you don't need to cover them all! These ideas are provided as food for thought—it is ultimately your call which categories should be represented in your box.

Accomplishments	Art	Beauty in all its forms
Acquaintances	Articles I found	Beliefs
Activism	interesting	Bible verses
Adventures	Articles I wrote	Birthday celebrations
Advice	Artifacts	Body image
Ancestors	Astrology	Books
Anecdotes	Aunts and uncles	Bosses
Animal friends	Awards	Boundaries I set
Anxieties	Bands I like	Bucket list

Bumps in the road

Camping

Camps

Cards

Cars and transportation

Celebrations

Charities and causes

Cherished objects

Childhood memories

Children

Clients

Coaches

Collections

College

Community

Competitions

Confrontations

Conversations that had
  an impact

Correspondence

Cousins

Coworkers

Cultural activities

Dating

Decisions

Diaries

Diets

Difficult choices

Disappointments

Distractions

Divorce

Documentaries

Documents relevant
  to supporting my life
  story

Donations

Downsizing

Drawings

Dreams

Education

Emails

Embarrassing moments

Engagement

Entertainment

Events

Experiences

Extended family

Failures

Faith

Falling in love

Family

Family stories

Fantasies

Fashion

Father

Favorites

Fears

Finances

Firsts

Fitness

Foods and beverages

Forgiveness

Friendship

Frustration

Fulfillment

Funny moments

Games

Gardening

Gifts

Goals

Grandchildren

Grandparents

Gratitude

Grief

Growing up

Happiness

Health

Heartbreaks

Heroes

High school

History-changing
  events in my lifetime

Hobbies

Holidays

Home

Honeymoon

Hopes

Hotels and resorts

House of worship

Humor

Ideas

Illusions

Impactful events

Impactful people

Indulgences

Inheritance

In-laws

Insights

Inspiration

Intentions

Inventions

Investments

Invitations

Itineraries

Jobs and job
  descriptions

Journals

Leadership

Legal documents

Lies

Life lessons

Life philosophy

Literature

Litigations

Liturgy

Losses

Love

Love letters

Luck

Lyrics

Marriage

Medical history

Meditations

Mementos

Memorabilia

Memories

Mental health

Mentors

Middle school

Milestones

Military

Mindfulness

Mistakes

Morals

Mother

Motto

Moves

Movies

Music

Natural disasters

Neighbors and
  neighborhoods

Newspaper clippings

Nieces and nephews

Nightmares

Nominations

Objects

Offices

Organizations I
  belong to

Outdoor activities

Parenthood

Partners

Passions and pastimes

Performance reviews

Performances

Perspectives

Pets

Philanthropy

Photographs

Places

Plays

Podcasts

Poems

Politics

Postcards

Pregnancies

Preschool

Professional life

Proposals

Proudest moments

Publications

Questions

Quotes

Recipes

Recordings

Recovery

Regrets

Religion

Report cards

Research

Resignations

Restaurants

Résumés

Retirement

Road trips

Role models

Romance

Routine

Sacrifice

Sadness

Satisfaction

Schedules

School

Secrets

Setbacks

Shows

Siblings

Social media

Sorrows

Special occasions

Speeches

Spirituality

Sports

Strengths

Struggles

Style

Superstitions

Talents

Teachers

Texts

Therapy

Toys

Traditions

Traits

Trauma

Travel

Trophies

Turning points

TV shows

Unanswered questions

Vacations

Values

Videos

Voicemails

Volunteerism

Weaknesses

Weather

Wedding

Will

Words of wisdom

Work and career

Workouts

Appendix 3

Additional Resources

———————

V isit www.oritramler.com to find helpful tips, articles, and resources that will aid in your boxing journey. You will also find ways to join and get inspired by a growing community of boxers.

Need help in creating your or a loved one's Box of Life? Are you interested in joining a workshop or hosting Orit at your organization? Contact us at orit@oritramler.com for coaching, guidance, and tips.

Acknowledgments

G ratitude is a virtue that needs to be put into action as often as possible. I want to thank those who helped make my first book a reality:

- My husband, who has always believed in me. He shared with everyone we interacted with that I was writing a book and gave me feedback and ideas along the way. Te amo, Gaby!

- My kids, who helped me with editing and taught me many rules of grammar in my second language. While doing so, I'm sure they added to their list of all the funny things I say in English. Maia and Ilan, you are the best I could ask for!

- My parents, who inspired me with their love and stories and kept encouraging me while understanding how busy I was with juggling life, work, and writing.

- My friends, who constantly asked for updates and encouraged me to keep going along the way. You know who you are!

- Capitán, my beloved Labrador who sat next to me every time

I wrote until the day he took his last breath. Capi, your paw is imprinted on my heart forever!

- My dog Addie, who seems to understand that I need to focus when I'm writing.
- The wonderful professionals who guided me and provided invaluable advice throughout this writing journey. Karin Wiberg, Margot Herrera, and the dedicated team at Amplify Publishing Group. Your expertise and encouragement have made this book possible.
- My coaching clients and those who shared their trust and stories with me. It is your journeys, challenges, and victories that breathed life into these pages. You reminded me every day why I embarked on this writing journey, and for that I am profoundly grateful.
- Ina Stern, for giving me her blessing and encouragement to publish this book.
- My beloved friend Charles Stern for inspiring me, believing in me, and providing me with the most meaningful project I could ask for.
- Life itself!

Me organizing Charles's mementos

About the Author

Orit Ramler is a seasoned entrepreneur and executive coach with over thirty years of experience in business, leadership, and personal and professional development. She is a globally sought-after coach and the founder of Make It a Good One® Coaching and Consulting, which focuses on client-centered coaching, and The Box of Life Project®, which helps individuals and organizations live with purpose while preserving their most valuable stories and memories. Orit's practice also draws on her previous outreach, leadership, and fundraising experience as an executive director for nonprofit organizations. She served on different boards, among them the Board of Visitors for the Duke University School of Nursing and coached for DELTA Leadership Inc. as part of Duke's FUQUA Business School Executive MBA Program.

Orit is a certified coach and holds a master's degree in educational psychology. She has lived in seven countries, giving her a unique understanding of culture and human behavior. She resides in Durham, North Carolina, where she loves spending time with her family, friends, and furry companions.